The Path of
Loneliness

The Path of Loneliness

Finding Your Way Through the Wilderness to God

Elisabeth Elliot

Revell
Grand Rapids, Michigan

© 1998, 2001 by Elisabeth Elliot

Published by Fleming H. Revell
a division of Baker Publishing Group
P.O. Box 6287, Grand Rapids, MI 49516-6287
www.revellbooks.com

New paperback edition published 2007
ISBN 10: 0-8007-3206-5
ISBN 978-0-8007-3206-6

Previously published in 1988 by O. Nelson and in 2001 by Servant Publications

Printed in the United States of America

The Library of Congress has cataloged the previous paperback edition as follows:
Elliot, Elisabeth.
    The path of loneliness : finding your way through the wilderness to God
/ Elisabeth Elliot.
        p.   cm.
    Originally published: Ann Arbor, Mich. : Vine Books, 2001.
    Includes bibliographical references.
    ISBN 10: 0-8007-5994-X (paper)
    ISBN 978-0-8007-5994-0 (paper)
    1. Loneliness—Religious aspects—Christianity. 2. Christian life.
3. Elliot, Elisabeth. I. Title.
BV4911.E54 2004
248.8'6—dc22   2004052301

In keeping with biblical principles of creation stewardship, Baker Publishing Group advocates the responsible use of our natural resources. As a member of the Green Press Initiative, our company uses recycled paper when possible. The text paper of this book is comprised of 30% post-consumer waste.

green press
INITIATIVE

To the memory of Katherine Morgan

Blessed are [those] whose strength is in thee,
in whose heart are the highways to Zion.
As they go through the valley of Baca
they make it a place of springs....
They go from strength to strength.
PSALM 84:5-7, RSV

Contents

Preface to the Second Edition

Readers will note that this book was originally published in 1988. Some of its contents may seem a bit dated. Nevertheless I believe that the topic of loneliness is of perennial interest to all of us at every season of our lives.

It is my earnest prayer that those who tread this path may find the companionship of One who calls Himself the God of peace. May you also discover what the apostle Paul learned while he was in prison: "I have learned the secret of being content in any and every situation, whether well fed or hungry, whether living in plenty or in want. I can do everything through him who gives me strength" (Phil. 4:12, 13, NIV).

Elisabeth Elliot

Acknowledgments

My sincere thanks are due
to those who gave permission to use their stories.

Chapter One

The Sudden Tide

It is midnight. Off the right wing of the plane the moon floods with light a vast field of clouds, like cobblestones. Inside the plane it is dark except for a few dim lights and the EXIT signs. The stewardess moves quietly up the aisle, taking a blanket to someone. The man and woman next to me are apparently asleep. They have been quiet for a long time. I try to fit my legs into the cramped space allotted, but they are too long. The seat is too narrow. The pillow is too small to cradle my head comfortably against the bulkhead. In spite of the deep thrum of the engines, smooth and regular, I can't sleep.

The woman beside me moves, opens her purse, finds something, leans back again. The man stirs. Neither says anything. There is a tiny click, then a clear flame, as the man reaches to light his companion's cigarette. I can see the outline of his hand, the knuckles and fingers, the hairs illuminated for a few seconds.

The woman draws, puffs a thin column of smoke. Another click. Darkness.

Only the most ordinary of gestures, meaning almost nothing, I suppose, to them. But for me, sitting there by the window looking out again at the cold stars, it speaks of a whole world that is lost to me now. A man and a woman. Together. His hand stretched toward her to help.

I am traveling alone. I am a widow. I remember another hand—a bit bigger than that one, with fingers strong for wrestling and carpentry, dexterous for drawing, tender for caressing. I can still see the square fingernails, and how the hair grew on the back of that hand. The man it belonged to has been gone more than a year, long enough for me to have difficulty remembering how it felt when he touched me, how it was to put my hand inside his.

I lean my forehead against the glass and a great heaving tide pours over me, drowns me—as it has done a hundred times in the past year. But there are so many so much worse off than I. I remember that. How blessed I have been, to have been a wife even for a short time. Yet, in the most unpremeditated ways, in the oddest places and for the most absurd reasons, as I'm going about my business, generally calm, even cheerful, that sudden tide sweeps in. It's called loneliness.

Fifteen years later I am a widow again. Most of my tears were shed before he died, as I watched cancer take him to pieces. The funeral is a celebration of joy—he is at peace, free at last from what he called his "vile body." We sing "Guide Me, O Thou

Great Jehovah," the hymn which has (except in the newer muti-lated versions) that wonderful line,

> Death of Death and Hell's Destruction,
> Land me safe on Canaan's side.

I do not feel at all like crying—except for joy at the thought of Christ's being the Death of Death. I did not cry at the memorial service for my first husband. It seemed very strange to onlookers, I'm sure—"She must be made of concrete!"—but I am not the only one who has experienced this. It often happens that those whose loss is greatest receive the greatest share of grace, mercy, and peace. This does not mean that they never cry, of course. But they do not collapse. Those who only watch and pray and try to put themselves in the place of the bereaved find it almost unendurable. Sometimes they weep uncontrollably, for their imaginations never include the grace.

So it happens for me at the funeral. The peace given simply passes understanding, and I am borne up by those intense prayers, as if on strong wings, far above grief.

But suddenly, one day as I am pulling something from the shelf in the supermarket, the tide sweeps in and I find myself sobbing. Happily no one seems to notice. If someone should, would my explanation ("My husband died three months ago") make sense to him—*here*, in the *supermarket*?

In order to get to the hotel dining room we have to walk past the disco bar. The noise is too loud to tell whether it's music or what. The smoke is too thick to see who's up there making the noise, but in the twirling mirrored lights we can see the writhing shapes on the dance floor. Male or female? I can't always tell by their dress. They're not touching. Their hands are moving back and forth in the air in front of them, their bodies gyrating, shaking, grinding. Occasionally one bumps a shoulder to remind another that he/she has a partner. A knot of men stands near the door. Four women sit sideways on bar stools, legs generously displayed, elbows on the bar, hands drooping over the rims of glasses, eyes ceaselessly scanning the room. There is loneliness in the eyes, the acute loneliness one senses, seeking one soul who might be an "answerer."

It's Saturday night. It's where the singles come in this cowtown west of the Mississippi.

We (a third husband and I) pause, watch the scene for a minute, go on by. We sit in the dining room, thankful for quiet, thankful that we need not join the lonely crowd. We have each other, and it's for life (a longer one this time, please God).

Why do they come? It can't possibly be for the food or for what passes for music. They haven't got dates. They are lonely hunters. What else do you do in Cowtown, or in New York, on a Saturday night—if you're lonely?

In Toronto, for example, according to an article in an airline magazine, we learn that there are other options. You can join a singles club, call a dating service, go to a dance club or a dining club, or, if you're "into" adult education, you can sign up for something called "culinary courtship," which lets you eat a progressive dinner every six weeks, with each of four courses consumed at a different table with five or six different faces. If you want to lay out $695 you can buy six introductions to members of the opposite (or, according to your "preference," the same) sex and be taught how to act, dress, and talk in can't-miss ways to lure them. For a cool $1,000 you can get your name on a list that gives you a chance (not a guarantee) to be called by the Rich and Famous, i.e., men who make $100,000 or more (the article did not define Famous).

In Birmingham a hostess pairs her party guests and has a uni-formed guard handcuff them together for the entire evening. "They had to swim and eat and do everything (except visits to the restroom) together," she reported, "but it never resulted in any permanent couplings."

Near our home in Massachusetts an enormous grocery emporium is sponsoring Singles Nights when the unattached can shop for food and each other. They call it the Meet Market.

The Personals columns of newspapers and magazines are a measure of the desperation men and women feel in their lone-liness.

What is to be done with loneliness?

Chapter Two

Fierceness and Tenderness

There is an answer, I believe, to the question asked at the end of the first chapter. But first we need to go back to the beginnings of things.

Paul Tillich, in *The Eternal Now*, writes,

Being alive means being in a body—a body separated from all other bodies. And being separated means being alone. This is true of every creature, and it is more true of man than of any other creature. He is not only alone; he also *knows* that he is alone.... This aloneness he cannot endure. Neither can he escape it. It is his destiny to be alone and to be aware of it. Not even God can take this destiny away from him.[1]

When God created the world He saw each thing that He made as good. But when He made man, He saw that it was not good that man should be alone. Man is a social creature like the animals. They move in pairs or flocks or herds. God designed the answer to Adam's aloneness: a woman. They were a couple, meant to answer to each other.

Each, however, was still alone in a profound sense—in a separate body, alone before God, bearing His image, answering to Him, responsible. This aloneness was a good thing, for everything in the Garden was perfect.

But something happened. Sin destroyed the perfect harmony of the universe. The relationship of man with God and of human beings with each other was fractured. Man now *knows* that he is alone. His aloneness is no longer an experience only of solitude (not by any means a bad thing in itself) but also of deprivation. The human companionship, which in the divine plan was the answer to man's aloneness, no longer suffices. Disobedience ruined it. His aloneness has another dimension which is an experience of pain—a pain called loneliness. This kind of pain is a part of what philosophers term "the human predicament," the character, status, or condition of humanity. No one ever escapes it.

Most of us, I suppose, have sensed our solitude especially poignantly on occasions when we have stood before the grandeur of nature—a roaring thunderstorm, a spangled midnight sky, a crashing sea. It can be comforting or it can be terrifying, depending on our relationship with the One who brought it all into being, or perhaps merely on the mood of the moment.

It is a terrible thing—and only if one were subhuman and brutish could it fail to be terrifying—to have no roots in this world, to be homeless, isolated, an "unplaced person," to be on the earth but not of it. What in the Old Testament figure of Melchizedech—"without father, without mother, without genealogy"—is mystery, for us would be tragedy. Without family or friends or foothold in the earth, without sun and stars and winds, we should be only half alive, doomed to at best a twilight existence; to be fully alive is to be in some way part of these things—and of their fierceness as of their tenderness.[2]

So writes Gerald Vann in *The Son's Course*. He has put his finger on the cause of greatest human desolation. We must have a foothold.

The world offers its poor anodynes and they are eagerly seized—"I *might* find the answer in the singles bar, the Personals column, the Meet Market." It is true indeed that the lonely might find a mate, someone willing to have a go at loving them, at least for a night, but is this really the answer they seek? Without a foothold, without an awareness of being a part of something grander and greater than themselves, it will not be enough.

It was the Love of God that brought us all into being—sun, stars, winds, men and women, and "infants to sweeten the world" (to use a phrase from an old prayer which I love). To know God, or even to begin to know Him, is to know that we are not alone in the universe. Someone Else is Out There. There is a hint that there may be a refuge for our loneliness. To stop our frantic getting, spending, and searching, and simply to *look* at the things God has made is to move one step away from despair. For God cares. The most awesome seascape can reveal a care which is actually *tender.*

"Who watched over the birth of the sea, when it burst in flood from the womb?" God asked Job in the midst of his great suffering, "when I wrapped it in a blanket of cloud and cradled it in fog?" (Job 38:8-9, NEB). A God who can look on the mighty ocean as a tiny newborn—could He overlook one of His lonely people? Job had felt very much overlooked. Yet, after all his questions and accusations, he was shown that not for a moment had he really been forgotten.

"Do you ... attend the wild doe when she is in labor? Do you count the months that they carry their young or know the time of their delivery, when they crouch down to open their wombs?" (Job 39:1-3, NEB). If God sees the doe in the throes of her agony and attends the delivery of her fawn in the forest, we may believe that an aching heart does not escape His notice.

To my father I owe a deep consciousness of God as Creator. I cannot remember a time when I was not aware of the songs of birds, the glory of mountains, the freshness of the dawn, the deep sweetness of a forest of white pines, the mystery of the night sky. He taught us to see, hear, smell, feel, taste. Both parents taught us in a thousand ways to know the One who made us all, and to trust Him. And they told us the story which, far more than all the glories of nature, opens the heart of God— the story of the One "who is the effulgence of God's splendour and the stamp of God's very being" (Heb. 1:3, NEB), the story of Jesus, His birth to a virgin-mother, His life, His death on the Cross. When we were very small they taught us to trust Him; they sang to us at bedtime, "Safe in the Arms of Jesus." That's where we grew up.

But safety, as the Cross shows, does not exclude suffering. All that was of course beyond me when I was a child, but as I began to learn about suffering I learned that *trust* in those strong arms means that even our suffering is under control. We are not doomed to meaninglessness. A loving Purpose is behind it all, a great tenderness even in the fierceness.

Chapter Three

Loneliness Is a Wilderness

One of the times when loneliness pours over us is when we are threatened by illness.

The phone rang late one night and a timid voice began to tell me, very hesitatingly, about a great perplexity. She was a new Christian. Things had been going wonderfully well and God had given her work to do for Him, but it was all going to grind to a halt because of illness which would probably lead to total incapacity.

"It seems very strange to me that God would allow this to happen," said the voice.

Of course it did. God's ways are mysterious indeed. Yet He tells us not to think them strange. Our temptations are common to man, His faithfulness is constant. I sent up an instant prayer for help in showing her what God might be up to. I had to try to start from her simple assumption, which seems logical enough, that God wants us to be happy. It is indeed true, but in a much deeper way than we think. "Happiness," as defined by the world, means exemption from suffering. As Peter Kreeft tells us in his masterful book, *Making Sense Out of Suffering*, ancient man was preoccupied with how to be good while modern man is preoccupied with how to be happy. To the ancient, goodness leads to happiness. To the modern, goodness leads to anything but. "Everything I enjoy is immoral, illegal, or fattening" is the saying.

I didn't weigh in with all of this to the troubled girl on the phone, but I did try to help her see that as a Christian she might look at things from a different angle. She needed to start from the Love of God and understand that that love, revealed on the Cross, does not exclude but must always *include* suffering.

"But what good will I be flat on my back?" came the plaintive question. So we had to talk about God's idea of "good"— very different from mere utilitarianism. He wanted her to trust and obey ("for there's no other way to be happy in Jesus," as the old gospel song says). The only way she could learn trust and obedience was to have things happen which she could not understand. That is where faith begins—in the wilderness, when you are alone and afraid, when things don't make sense.... She must hang onto the message of the Cross: God loves you. He loved you enough to die for you. Will you trust Him?

I gave her St. Peter's word about the trial of faith being a more precious thing than gold—and even gold has to go through fire to be purified. Fire is hot. Fire causes pain. But a pure faith would be worth far more to God than all the service she had hoped to render if poor health had not interrupted her plans.

There was a pause. Then I heard the timid little voice say, "Oh." I'm sure she felt she was about to enter a waste, howling wilderness and she was afraid. I prayed that God would go with her every step of the way and let her know that everything was under control.

Suffering is a wilderness experience. We feel very much alone and helpless, cut off from others who cannot know how we suffer. We long for someone to come to our aid, be "company" for us, get us out of this.

Someone will. Some One will certainly come to our aid. He will be company for us if we'll let Him. But get us out of it? Not necessarily. It is one of the terms of being human (which means that although we cannot do anything *about* it, there is something very important that we can do *with* it—but more of that later). Jesus Himself, being a man subject to all of a man's temptations, was not excused from the wilderness experience.

It was immediately after His Baptism, when it would seem He was all ready to begin His public ministry. Instead of to Jerusalem where He would be able to "reach" crowds, the Spirit of God led Him straight to a place where there was nobody—a wilderness—for the express purpose of being put to the test. The test came in the form of an encounter with Satan. And so it does with us. When we are hungry, cut off from help, and alone, the enemy comes to meet us. He makes what's right seem unattractive and what's wrong seem very attractive. He offered Jesus everything the world counts essential to *happiness:*

the satisfaction of physical desire, immunity from danger, and "all the kingdoms of the world in their glory" (Matt. 4:8, NEB), which I take to mean everything else the world has to offer.

Jesus was tempted. The price of Satan's offers, on the face of it, was cheap—work a couple of small miracles, do obeisance to him. The price of obedience to the Father, on the other hand, was high. It would cost Him everything. Here was the real test of Jesus' trust, of His love for God, the purity of His purpose, the irrevocability of His commitment. He categorically refused every offer, meeting the test with the written Word:

It is written.

It is written.

It is written.

Satan knew he was vanquished and left.

I remember waking up very early one morning in a tiny reed-and-leaf shelter on the banks of the Curaray River. My three-year-old and I had spent the night there with some Indians on our way home to a clearing about a day's journey beyond. Rain was sweeping over the river and the sandy beach in great waving sheets, and with the rain a huge loneliness seemed about to drown me. I felt that I could not face a day like that in a dugout canoe, nor did I have the least desire to get back to that clearing. Civilization was what I wanted at that moment, not adventure, but I had no choice. God met me there that morning, and strengthened me with an *It is written,* reminding me of His promises, *I will never leave you nor forsake you. I am with you always* (Heb. 13:5, NEB; Matt. 28:20, KJV).

In the wilderness of loneliness we are terribly vulnerable.

What we want is OUT, and sometimes there appear to be some easy ways to get there. Will we take Satan up on his offers, satisfy our desires in ways never designed by God, seek security outside of His holy will? If we do, we may find a measure of happiness, but not the lasting joy our heavenly Father wants us to have. We will "gain the world," but we'll lose our souls. Jesus knew that His joy lay in only one direction: the will of the Father. And so does ours.

Pain, as C.S. Lewis said, is God's megaphone ("He whispers to us in our joys, speaks to us in our conscience, and shouts to us in our pain"). The pain of loneliness is one way in which He wants to get our attention.

We may be earnestly desiring to be obedient and holy. But we may be missing the fact that it is *here*, where we happen to be at this moment and not in another place or another time, that we may learn to love Him—here where it seems He is not at work, where His will seems obscure or frightening, where He is not doing what we expected Him to do, where He is most absent. Here and nowhere else is the appointed place. If faith does not go to work *here*, it will not go to work at all.

Is the response of faith really different from the response of the rest of the world? I want to tell you a story which shows that it is as different as night and day. It is the story of a man who was acutely lonely. His loneliness was the same stuff everybody suffers in one form or another. What this man did with it is something else.

Chapter Four

The Pain of Rejection

A hundred years ago a man's experience of desolation gave birth to a hymn which has been for me and for many the balm of heaven. George Matheson went blind shortly after becoming engaged. His fiancée broke the engagement.

Perhaps there is no more bitter loneliness than that of rejection. Not only must one learn to do without someone he had come to feel he could not live without, but he must endure dagger-thrusts to the heart, such as: You deserved to be rejected. You are not worthy to be loved. You will never be loved. Who would want you? You are condemned to loneliness forever, and nobody cares.

Fear and anger arise. If I turn to God *He* might reject me. How can I turn to Him anyway? He could have prevented this from happening. What else is He likely to do to me?

The devastating conclusion is reached: *I am alone.*

Matheson's grief, instead of turning to bitter resentment against the lady who had caused it, was transformed. Totally *transformed*. These profound and simple words show how that happened:

> O Love that wilt not let me go,
> I rest my weary soul in Thee;
> I give Thee back the life I owe,
> That in Thine ocean depths its flow
> May richer, fuller be.
>
> O Light that followest all my way,
> I yield my flickering torch to Thee;
> My heart restores its borrowed ray,
> That in Thy sunshine's blaze its day
> May brighter, fairer be.
>
> O Joy that seekest me through pain,
> I cannot close my heart to Thee;
> I trace the rainbow through the rain,
> And feel the promise is not vain
> That morn shall tearless be.
>
> O Cross that liftest up my head,
> I dare not ask to fly from Thee;
> I lay in dust life's glory dead,
> And from the ground there blossoms red
> Life that shall endless be.

What, exactly, did Matheson do? He gave back his life, restored the light of his life, opened his heart, laid down life's glory. That spells surrender, which can only come of trust.

His blindness and rejection proved to be for George Matheson the very means of illuminating the Love of God. He may have asked the age-old question, *Why?*, but God's answer is always *Trust Me*. Matheson turned his thoughts away from the woman he had lost, away from the powerful temptations to self-pity, resentment, bitterness toward God, skepticism of His Word, and selfish isolation which might so quickly have overcome him, and lifted up his "weary soul" to a far greater Love—one that would never let him go.

In the words "I give Thee back the life I owe" Matheson understood that there was *something he could do* with his suffering. It was the great lesson of the Cross: surrender. If Jesus had been unwilling to surrender to humanity's worst crime, humanity's salvation would have been impossible. But at Calvary the Lord of the Earth surrendered Himself into the hands of evil men. Yet, paradoxically, no one took His life from Him. He laid it down of His own will, offered Himself to the Father, "poured out His soul unto death," became broken bread and poured-out wine for the life of the world. We live because He died. The power of the Cross is not exemption from suffering but the very transformation of suffering.

Christianity is not a complete coverage insurance policy. Jesus suffered "not that we might not suffer," wrote George MacDonald, "but that our sufferings might be like His."

The Way of the Cross for George Matheson was heartbreak. God's power could have spared him that, but God's love chose instead to give him something far more precious than the happiness he had lost—the Oil of Joy. God gives that oil to those who need it, to those who mourn. Its price, in other words, is mourning. If he had not entered the lonely wilderness, George Matheson would not have found His sweet treasure. Would you say the price of *that* was too high? Your answer depends on where you set your sights—on the short range or the long one. Think what Matheson would have missed. Think what the world would have missed had he been given the form of happiness he hoped for. Denied that, he looked for something better. God never denies us our heart's desire except to give us something better.

With what misgivings we turn over our lives to God, imagining somehow that we are about to lose everything that matters. Our hesitancy is like that of a tiny shell on the seashore, afraid to give up the teaspoonful of water it holds lest there not be enough in the ocean to fill it again. Lose your life, said Jesus, and you will find it. Give up, and I will give you all. Can the shell imagine the depth and plenitude of the ocean? Can you and I fathom the riches, the fullness, of God's love?

In his blindness, Matheson must have thought a great deal about light.

> O Light that followest all my way,
> I yield my flickering torch to Thee.

A flickering torch—must he sacrifice his single source of light? He yields. When his heart "restores its borrowed ray," what happens? In place of his own dim torch he is given God's "sunshine's blaze."

Because the thing that he longed for, the joy of his life, was gone, he cried out in his desperation to another joy, to the Source of Joy itself:

O Joy that seekest me through pain.

I wonder if, for a moment or two, he might have felt as I sometimes do: I will not relinquish this misery, not right now. God has taken away what I most wanted. I have a right to feel sorry for myself. I have been wronged. I will refuse, for a while at least, any offer of comfort and healing. Don't speak to me of *joy*. You pour salt in my wounds. Let me lick them for a while.

If any such quite natural thoughts entered Matheson's mind, God understood, for He too had been a man. In His mercy He helped him to put them away and to write,

I cannot close my heart to Thee.

That is the response of a humbled heart, one that admits its poverty and recognizes the gentle Love that waits, the Joy that is seeking *him* precisely because he is in such pain that he can hardly seek anything but death. Then, although he is blind, he sees with the eye of faith, and what he sees, through the mist of his tears, is a rainbow. He comes to believe that the promise is true: Tears are not forever. There will be a morning without them. His faith lays hold of the promise and, mysteriously, he finds that pain has been exchanged for joy. If he had closed his heart and indulged his feelings, he might have found some miserably meager happiness, but he would have forfeited the joy.

"If God loves me, He'll make me happy." Well, yes and no. Happy isn't the word, really. It's joy, a far better thing. Not sentiment, not mere "feeling good," but something that can never be taken away.

Love, Light, Joy. There is yet something else that the God who is Love and the Father of Lights and the Source of all Joy wants to give him. It is the Cross. Will he accept that? It can always be evaded, but if it is, the result is endless loss. His answer:

> O Cross that liftest up my head,
> *I dare not* ask to fly from Thee.

By this time he understands what he would be rejecting. With both hands, as it were, he takes it, says YES, surrenders, lays everything he holds dear—"life's glory"—down in the dust.

And what happens? Is that the end of the story? No. A thousand times No. Out of that sterile dust springs a miracle:

> And from the ground there blossoms red
> Life that shall endless be.

Chapter Five

All My Desire
Is Before Thee

O ne summer evening in 1949 I was sitting on a rustic bench
on the side of Mount Tabor in Portland, Oregon. At a
respectful distance beside me sat the man I loved and longed
with all my soul to marry. More than a year had passed since he
had confessed his love for me. It appeared that the missionary
work to which each of us had been called might require that we
remain single.

This man, like my father, loved all of God's outdoors, saw in
it the overwhelming evidence of His power and the lavish gifts
of His love. We revelled in it together. There was a warm
breeze, filled with the warm fragrance of Douglas firs. The lights
of the city winked below us, and beyond them in the moonlight
stood the luminous majesty of Mount Hood.

"Happy the race of men, if that love were to rule your hearts
which rules the heavens!" wrote Boethius from the dungeon

where he awaited his death in the fifth century. I wanted to be ruled by that Love, but found myself in danger of being ruled by a lesser.

Although I don't think the word occurred in our conversation that evening, it was the undercurrent of all we talked about: loneliness. I would soon be leaving for home in New Jersey. Would we ever meet again? When? Where? Were we to be single forever? *Please, Lord, no,* my heart was saying, *I will die without him.* I knew in my head that God's love would never give less than the best. My heart was convinced that marriage to this man was "the best," but my head argued that my heart might be mistaken. I still wanted what God wanted to give—nothing more, nothing less, nothing else. Was I deceiving myself? Would I still submit to the rule of the Love that rules the heavens?

These were the things going through my mind. I kept most of them to myself, however, determined to bare my feelings to no man until he had proposed—and even then to be extremely cautious, for an emotional striptease leads to a physical one far more quickly than most of us are prepared for.

Jim pointed out something in the Bible I had not noticed before. I was startled by it.

"Everyone has his own particular gift from God, some one thing and some another."

There he goes again, I thought, *quoting Scripture.* Jim Elliot was a walking Bible. Knew it backwards and forwards, and was forever nailing me with verses exactly suited to pierce to the very marrow.

"Ever think about that one, Betts?" he said. "Singleness is a gift. 'To those who are unmarried or widowed, I say definitely that it is a good thing to remain unattached, as I am' (1 Cor. 7:7-8, PHILLIPS). That's the apostle Paul talking."

It sounded like him all right. Not very palatable just now. Singleness, if it was a gift, held no attraction for me. I was nearly twenty-three and my friends were getting married in rapid succession. I, only I, was left. And here beside me, on this lovely evening in this idyllic place, living and breathing (I was tinglingly aware even of his breathing), sat the man I would give anything in the world to marry. But was he asking me to marry him? Nothing of the sort. He was asking me to see my solitary status as a *gift*.

My call to missionary work was certainly a gift. It was a vocation and a privilege. But celibacy? That was a vocation for nuns. I hardly thought of it as a privilege, and who besides nuns would call it a gift? If it was any of those things for me, I devoutly hoped it would not last a lifetime.

Years before that talk on Mount Tabor I had made up my mind that I wanted one thing beyond all things: I wanted to know Christ. By the time I was twelve I had read *Pilgrim's Progress* and many missionary stories, and was aware that this ambition was going to cost me something. I began slowly to learn that Christ can be known only in the path of obedience. "Every man who knows my commandments and obeys them is the man who really loves me, and every man who really loves me will himself be loved by my Father, and I too will love him and *make myself known* to him." (John 14:17, PHILLIPS, italics added).

Obedience proves love, and love opens the heart to

knowledge. Never a day goes by that does not bring fresh opportunities to know Him—if only we will do what He says. It is easy enough to give assent to the principle, once it is pointed out. It is not so easy to recognize our chance to put it into practice, especially when that chance comes in an unpalatable form. This huge unfulfilled desire—a means for knowing Christ? I could not see it that way.

"The path of obedience" meant missionary life for me. I felt sure of that, and embraced the prospect with joy. My eagerness was not unmixed with ignoble motives—it's nice to think you may do something for God and be admired for it. But now another issue nettled me: What if obedience meant not just missionary life but Old Maid missionary life?

I crept quietly to bed that night so as not to waken Jane, Jim's sister who shared her room with me. I lay awake, having a silent dialogue with the Lord. He seemed to be asking,

"What do you want more than anything else in the world?"

Jim Elliot was the first answer that sprang to mind. But I had not forgotten my ten-year commitment (God help me, I could not change it). Hoping I spoke the truth, I answered, "To know You, Lord."

"Do you want My will, at any cost?"

The truth, the whole truth, nothing but the truth couldn't pull any wool over God's eyes. Was it yes to this question?

"Yes, Lord."

About two years earlier, before I had known of Jim's attraction to me, I had written:

Perhaps some future day, Lord, Thy strong hand
Will lead me to the place where I must stand
Utterly alone.

Alone, O Gracious Lover, but for Thee;
I shall be satisfied if I can see
Jesus only.

I do not know Thy plan for years to come,
My spirit finds in Thee its perfect home,
Sufficiency.

Lord, all my desire is before Thee now,
Lead on, no matter where, no matter how—
I trust in Thee.

As well as I could, I laid all my desire once more before Him
to whom all desire is known and from whom no secrets are hidden. The next day I boarded a bus for Philadelphia with no
guarantee that I would see Jim again.

Chapter Six

The Gift of
Widowhood

For four more years after that evening on Mount Tabor singleness was the gift God was giving me. Like all of His gifts, it was appropriate to the job He had assigned and I tried to accept it gladly. I embarked alone on a freighter to Ecuador, South America, studied Spanish, and then went to work in the western jungle, reducing to writing an unwritten Indian language. Jim was doing similar work in another tribe on the other side of the Andes.[1]

On October 8, 1953, there was a new assignment and a new gift. It was a brilliant morning in the capital city, Quito, the City of Eternal Spring. I was nearly exploding with joy when I happened to meet a missionary friend just up from the western jungle. He chatted about the business he needed to attend to that day, then asked, "And what are you doing?"

"Well," said I, "among other things, I'm getting married this morning at ten o'clock."

I was about to become Mrs. P. James Elliot. What an assignment!

This was the condition and context of the will of God for me now—and for the rest of my life, I thought. "Till death us do part" sounded like a long time.

It wasn't so long. Twenty-seven months later there was another assignment.

*   *   *

Five wives and nine children under seven years old waited in Shell Mera, Ecuador, for news of five men who were in the territory of a hostile tribe of Indians with whom they hoped to make friends and open the way for missionary work. Radio contact had been lost. The men were missing.

Life had to go on. Hordes of people had come to help and had to be given food and beds. Babies had to be fed and changed, hundreds of diapers washed (no Pampers in those days). Marj Saint, ever efficient, managed everything. Her house was the center of Operation Auca. Her husband the pilot was missing, and she sat hour after hour at the radio, waiting for word from the rescue parties. In between helping the other wives with guests and babies, I ransacked my Bible for promises that Jim would come back. I found one which I hopefully applied: "Jacob shall return, and shall be in rest, and be quiet" (Jer. 30:10, KJV). I knew that Jacob was the Hebrew form of James. To this I added the psalmist's prayer, "Remember the word unto thy servant, upon which thou hast caused me to hope" (Ps. 119:49, KJV), and the verse my dear spiritual mother, Mom Cunningham, always gave me in her letters: "The God of hope fill you with all joy and peace in believing" (Rom. 15:13, KJV). I was putting together a neat package on which to pin my faith.

We waited, hanging on for dear life to every shred of hope of any kind. At last a radio message: "One body, sighted from the plane."

"Sit still, my daughter," I wrote in my journal (quoting the word of Naomi to Ruth). Then again, "Jacob shall return."

"Another body." Whose? we wanted to know. Unidentified.

The United States Air Force sent a rescue squad from Panama. As the C-47 circled the site, reporting to us in Shell Mera by radio, I wrote, "3:20 P.M. Yea, in the way of thy judgments, O Lord, have we waited for thee; the desire of our soul is to thy name, and to the remembrance of thee" (Isa. 26:8, KJV).

The minutes were hours to us. Ten minutes later I noted down the words of Elisabeth to her cousin Mary, "Blessed is she that believed" (Luke 1:45, KJV).

Another half hour crawled by. "4:00 P.M. Still circling. Hope thou in God, for I shall yet praise Him" (Ps. 42:5, KJV).

Finally we knew. The men were dead. All five of them.

* * *

I was not a wife anymore. I was a widow. Another assignment. Another gift.

Don't imagine for a moment that that was the thought that occurred to me the instant the word came. *O Lord* was probably all I could think, stunned as we all were.

One step at a time over the years, as I sought to plumb the mystery of suffering (which cannot be plumbed), I began to see that there is a sense in which everything is a gift, even my widowhood. I hope I can explain.

There would be no widowhood if there were no death. The

Bible calls death an enemy. There would be no divorce if there were no sin. Sin is enmity against God. When sin entered the world through what theologians call the Fall of Man, death and all kinds of suffering followed. Because Adam and Eve took the word of the Serpent ("You will not die") as more trustworthy than the word of God ("You will surely die"), they ate forbidden fruit. That Declaration of Independence, a prideful defiance of what they were created to be, had consequences that affect every human being who has ever lived.

But God still loves us. This we know, for the Bible tells us so. C.S. Lewis wrote,

> In awful and surprising truth, we are the objects of His love. You asked for a loving God: you have one. The great spirit you so lightly invoked, the "lord of terrible aspect," is present: not a senile benevolence that drowsily wishes you to be happy in your own way, not the cold philanthropy of a conscientious magistrate, nor the care of a host who feels responsible for the comfort of his guests, but the consuming fire Himself, the Love that made the worlds, persistent as the artist's love for his work and despotic as a man's love for a dog, provident and venerable as a father's love for a child, jealous, inexorable, exacting as love between the sexes.[2]

That inexorable Love had allowed me to become a widow. But "allowed me to become" is not adequate. It even seems feeble to me now, for the Lord of Hosts is absolutely sovereign. He holds power over the universe, He holds authority over my life—not because He usurps the rights with which He endowed me in creation, but because I had specifically asked Him to be Lord of my life. I had prayed as earnestly as a child and a teenager and a woman can pray, *Thy will be done.* The coming of this transcendent authority into one's life is bound to be an active thing, an immense disruption at times.

This was one of those times. He had done more than merely "allow" a thing to "happen" *to* me. I do not know any more accurate way of putting it than to say that He had given me something. He had given me a gift—widowhood.

How can I say such a thing?

He does not whisk us at once to Glory. We go on living in a fractured world, suffering in one way or another the effects of sin—sometimes our own, sometimes others'. Yet I have come to understand even suffering, through the transforming power of the Cross, as a gift, for in this broken world, *in* our sorrow, He gives us Himself; *in* our loneliness, He comes to meet us, as in George Matheson's He came as the Love that would never let him go.

In His death Jesus Christ gave us life. The willingness of the Son of God to commit Himself into the hands of criminals became the greatest gift ever given—the Bread of the world, in mercy broken. Thus the worst thing that ever happened became the best thing that ever happened.

It can happen with us. At the Cross of Jesus our crosses are changed into gifts.

The Love that calls us into being, woos us to Himself, makes us His bride, lays down His life for us, and daily crowns us with lovingkindness and tender mercy, will *not,* no matter how it may appear in our loneliness, abandon us. "I will never [the Greek has five different negatives here], never, never, never, never leave you nor forsake you." (See Hebrews 13:5.)

When I speak of the "gift" of widowhood, I do not mean that God made us widows. He did not inspire the Auca Indians to throw their lances, and then see to it that they found their mark. He does not give people cancer, cause a baby to be born with deformities, or persuade husbands and wives to divorce.

These are among the evils which result from man's decision to disobey. In the Garden of Eden he chose death, as God had plainly told him beforehand. We are still just as free to choose, and the consequences are just as inexorable—but *so is His love.*

Chapter Seven

Under the Same
Auspices

Two days after I knew of Jim's death I took my baby Valerie
and went back to Shandia, our jungle station.

Volume 6 of my journal had encompassed all of the months
of marriage. It was a slim volume. Now it was time to start a
new one. There was no stationery store where I could buy a
notebook, so I pulled out the old looseleaf I had used in college
and turned to the last entry, written in what was then my habit-
ual style, saturated with the English of the King James Bible:

> Lord, I do once more acknowledge, with all my heart, that *I
> am Thine.* No claim have I upon this life, past, present, or
> future. I am all, all Thine own. Thou hast said, "Fear not; for
> I have redeemed thee, I have called thee by thy name; *thou
> art mine....* I will be with thee.... I am the Lord thy God....
> I have loved thee.... I am with thee" (Isa. 43:1-5, KJV).
> Therefore, O dear Lord and Master, Redeemer, Lover,
> Friend, Beloved, do Thou work out Thine entire will in my
> life henceforth at any cost, in the time that is left to me on
> this earth. How short that may be I do not know at all, but

I trust Thee. "Thy testimonies have I taken as a heritage for ever: for they are the rejoicing of my heart." "He *shall* preserve thy soul" (Pss. 119:111, 121: 7, KJV).

When I wrote that on my twenty-fourth birthday (I was now twenty-nine), I had no inkling of the form the answer was to take.

In Shandia I sat down at the desk Jim had built in the corner of our bedroom, looking out through the screen toward the small clearing, surrounded by deep forest. In the adjoining room Valerie was asleep on a little wooden bed with a lumpy cotton mattress. It was the last piece of furniture Jim had made. I began to write on the next blank page of the old, college looseleaf notebook:

> Life begins a new chapter—this time without Jim ... I have been reading over some of the first part of this book—it is almost prophetic. They were days when God was teaching me to find satisfaction in Himself, without Jim. But always there was the hope that some day He would give us to one another. He did, on October 8, 1953. Two years and three months together.

> If Thy dear Home be fuller, Lord,
> For that a little emptier
> My house on earth, what rich reward
> That guerdon were.
>
> Amy Carmichael[1]

These words come to me over and over. The peace which I have received is certainly beyond all understanding.

As I went about my work in the house, on the station, with the Indians, I found peace as I looked up to the Father of Lights, from whom comes "every good endowment and every complete gift" (Jas. 1:17, PHILLIPS).

I say that I found peace. I do not say that I was not lonely. I was—terribly. I do not say that I did not grieve. I did—most sorely. But peace of the sort the world cannot give comes, not by the removal of suffering, but in another way—through acceptance. I was learning that the same Lord, in whom there is "never the slightest variation or shadow of inconsistency" (Jas. 1:17, PHILLIPS), the Lord who had given me singleness and marriage as gifts of His love, had now given me this one. Would I receive it from His hand? Would I thank Him for it?

I began to go deeper into the lesson of college days—that of finding satisfaction in Christ, apart from the man I hungered for. That was a gift I could not have received in any context other than the loneliness of being single. Now that Jim was dead, I had to repeat the lesson. It was more difficult this time, for there was no hope of my having him.

Amy Carmichael's words, "a little emptier my house on earth," held new meaning now, for I had what I had not had in college, a home of my own, the house Jim had designed and built, furnished with the fairly crude but functional things he had made, every corner redolent of his personality and presence. That house seemed empty now—but empty (so I trusted and prayed) that the Lord's house might be fuller. Of course I had my baby—a gift unspeakably lovely when she first arrived, even more precious now as Jim's legacy, the fruit of our love, a heavenly gift of comfort and joy. If I had not been widowed I would never have seen my house or my child in quite that light.

Had I asked above all to know God? He had been answering that prayer all along—in the single years, in the blessings of marriage and motherhood. It was time to find Him in the Valley of the Shadow of Death.

*   *   *

Widowhood taught me another kind of loneliness. My social life was for the most part limited to Quichua Indian friends. I had never been anything but a misfit with Indians, being so incorrigibly white and tall and foreign, but I was used to that and so were they. We all took it as a great source of amusement. I was not quite so amused to discover, on the rare occasions when I joined other missionaries, that I was now a misfit with them too. In some ways all single people are misfits in society, just as someone who has lost a leg is handicapped. God meant for everybody to have two legs apiece. We don't notice them when they are both there, but if one is missing, it's noticeable.

God's design for men and women was marriage. Sin and death distorted that design. Public education is now seeking to make community rather than family the basic social unit, because "family" in the traditional sense has become an oddity. We still remember what God meant by family: a mother and a father and the children which they *together* have produced. This kind of family has become so unusual it has had to be given a name—the "nuclear" family, which makes up only a small percentage of what the Internal Revenue Service calls a household.

In spite of this modern shuffling of ancient norms, social

gatherings are still often made up of what we (sometimes loosely) call couples. As a widow I never enjoyed being a fifth wheel. I threw things off balance simply by being there, but this was a reality I had to come to terms with. It was nobody's fault. It would be silly to protest that the married people were supposed to *do* something about my feelings in the matter. Many of them tried. Everybody was kindness itself in the beginning, hovering over me, offering help of all sorts, inviting me out. Many continued to be kind when the so-called grieving process was supposed to be over, but there was nothing in the world they could do about my not being half of a couple anymore.

So who could do something about it? God could, of course, if He wanted to give me another husband, but I had no right to expect a miracle. Was there anything *I* could do? There is always plenty of advice around about how to capture a husband. I did not plan to try. What I did plan to do was to accept the place God was giving me. As a widow I was still a member of the same Body. Christ was its Head, and God's great purpose had not been altered by my having lost a husband. It was a part of the plan.

Like the border collies that my friend Vergil Holland trains to herd sheep, I did not understand the pattern. The dogs have no idea what the master is up to with the flock. They only know one thing: obedience. I felt confused and insecure about my "place" now. There were practical matters which were going to take a good deal of learning, such as how to be a single parent and how to guide the young church Jim had left behind. My duties as wife, mother, teacher, and Bible translator had been well-defined before, but the list had lengthened considerably.

Many years ago my father was the associate editor of a Christian magazine of which his uncle was editor. When Uncle Charlie died my father was overwhelmed with his new responsibility as editor. The words my grandfather wrote to him then have helped me greatly: "We are still under the same Auspices."

God in His sovereign will had given me a new place. I could accept that place, with all its new responsibilities and bafflements, assured that "the Lord himself goes at your head; he will be with you; he will not fail you or forsake you. Do not be discouraged or afraid" (Deut. 31:8, NEB).

That strong promise cheered me on. The Auspices under which I worked had not changed. For each day's demands, I found that the old rule, inscribed in an ancient parsonage in England, was my salvation: *Doe the Nexte Thinge*. As I tried to put that rule into shoe-leather, as it were, taking each duty quietly as the will of God for that moment, I no longer felt like a misfit.

Chapter Eight

Divorce:
The Ultimate Humiliation

Among the many letters I received after Jim's death came one from a college classmate of his, telling me how her husband (a missionary) had walked into the kitchen one day with the grocery bags, banged them down on the counter, said, "I'm leaving you," turned on his heel, and walked out the door. She wanted me to be aware that there are much worse ways of losing a husband than death. I have never had any doubt about that.

Divorce is a terrible thing. I should think divorced people would hate it almost as much as God does. But it is happening all the time, smashing families and individual lives to bits, and creating chaos in church and society. Since I have not walked that road, I asked permission to use the following letter from another who has. It came on a card on which were printed the words of Psalm 68:6, NASB: "God makes a home for the lonely."

I was reading the Psalms one night when I really saw that verse for the first time. I was still making the adjustment to coming home to an empty apartment at night and I was more scared than I wanted to admit.... There were no notes waiting when I opened the door, no signs of life, and worst of all, no one expecting me. The reality was beginning to sink in: despite friends and family who cared about me, I was essentially *alone* for the first time in my life.

So I was surprised—even shocked—to see my situation right there in print. *God makes a home for the lonely.* How? It seemed to me to be a rather bold statement. Yet I knew from experience that God does not make empty promises.

When we think of being lonely, we usually mean that there are no people around; no one with us, no one to talk to. Or else we find that the people around us are "not on our wavelength"—they don't understand us, and that can be worse than no company at all. So loneliness in my experience is not relieved by just anyone's company. It needs to be someone special—someone who understands me, someone who can listen and *be there when I need them*. It was this last part that forced me to confront the depth of my own loneliness. Of all my friends, no one person could be with me all the time. And even if they could, none of them had the power to do anything about my situation. It was ultimately my problem.

Yet here was the Bible saying that God could do something about my loneliness. As a matter of fact, if you look at the rest of the psalm, it says that God can "do something" about a lot of things. Nothing is too hard for Him. The psalmist goes on to elaborate from history exactly what that means: God is always on the side of His people in their battle for survival; from the massive exodus from Egypt to the individual plight of widows and orphans. He cares about justice. He is full of mercy. The giant scope of His power in world affairs does not cause Him to overlook our individual concerns. And He has come to earth to prove it. Because of that He can sympathize with our weakness. He understands our feelings because being human, He has experienced loneliness too.

Here's a Person who not only understands me but who fascinates me—a Person whom I have become thrilled to know. Christ calls me out of my natural self-centeredness by listening to my cries and then showing me the bigger picture. The better I come to know Him, the more I become interested in what He is interested in—the more I live and breathe for His Kingdom to come, for things to be done on earth as they are in heaven.

As the time of year approaches when we begin talking about going home for the holidays, these things become even more real to me. Where is my home ultimately? My home is where Christ is. My apartment has become a home because I share it with Him. As I have worked to make it a comfortable place to be, I have discovered new ways of expressing the gift of hospitality that He has nurtured in me through the years. God has made a home for me in order for me to share that home with others.

"God makes a home for the lonely" can also be translated

"God sets the lonely in families." Through the last year I have come to know the reality of a much bigger family than my own natural family, dear as they are to me. My larger family are those who also know Christ in an intimate way. They are the ones who have listened to my cries and at the same time encouraged me to consider issues larger than myself. They are the ones whom God has used not only to relieve my loneliness, but to deepen my love for the kingdom. As I find my place of service within the community of God's people, there is little time left to feel lonely!

My joy is becoming less dependent upon my own immediate circumstances and more attached to what He is doing. As limited as my understanding is now, I know that He is a God who never loses, a God who has taken the ultimate humiliation and defeat and turned it inside out. Somehow my ruined plans fit into His larger plans. And so in the moments when I am forced to face my own loneliness, I find that I am not really alone at all!

It is good to hear things said by more than one witness. I am so glad Bonnie's letter came just at the right time to be included here. She and I have been reading the same Book, have found its truth transforming. God is in the business of "turning things inside out."

This illustrates just what I want to say about the *gift* of loneliness. Bonnie's has become not only a gift for her (look at the spiritual gains), but, like all God's gifts, a gift for the rest of us—the people who share her hospitality, for example, and the people whom she is now able to console, including you and me.

She testifies that she no longer has much time to brood about it, a present-day corroboration of Paul's words to the Roman Christians:

> We can be full of joy here and now even in our trials and troubles. These very things will give us patient endurance; this in turn will develop a mature character, and a character of this sort produces a steady hope, a hope that will never disappoint us.
>
> ROMANS 5:3-5, PHILLIPS

If God had eliminated the problem He would have eliminated the particular kind of blessing which it bears. If Bonnie had not taken her troubles in the right spirit she would have missed that blessing. By acceptance she was laying her will alongside His, willing to cooperate, willing to put herself in the yoke with Him. It sounds to me as though she is actually finding that His yoke, so burdensome if borne all alone, is light. She has found that acceptance brings peace.

Chapter Nine

A Love Strong Enough to Hurt

The loss of someone we love, whether by death or otherwise, brings us to the brink of the abyss of mystery. If we wrestle, as most of us are forced to do, with the question of God in the matter, we are bound to ask why He found it necessary to withdraw such a good gift. We will not get the whole answer, but certainly one answer is the necessity of being reminded that wherever our treasure is there will our hearts be also. If we have put all our eggs in the basket of earthly life and earthly affections we haven't much left when the basket falls. Christians, being citizens of Another Country, subjects of a Heavenly King, are supposed to set their affections there rather than here—a lesson few learn without mortal anguish.

Sheldon Vanauken's love for his wife Davy, as he writes in *A Severe Mercy*, was an all-consuming love—passionate, romantic, and, as his friend C.S. Lewis pointed out to him, selfish. In their pre-Christian days a shortsighted view of happiness led them to exclude all others, to the point of Vanauken's refusal even to allow children to "mar" what he and Davy had. When they became Christians he began to feel that she was "holier than necessary," and to see God as his rival. One night Davy offered up her life for her husband, that his soul might be fulfilled.

Had they not had all anyone could ask for *fulfillment?* Davy knew they had not. She had found hers in Christ, and longed that her husband too should find his there. It was a drastic prayer she prayed, one that she knew would cost her something. It did. God accepted her surrender, and a year later she died.

A strange answer, some would say. The end of a "perfect" marriage. Stripped at last of the object of a passion that had shut out all else, Vanauken did, through much anguish, find the fulfillment for which Davy had prayed. Her death was what his friend Lewis called a severe mercy.

Might God sometimes take from us our love because we love too much? I don't think so. Surely it is impossible to love "too much," for love is from God, who *is* Love. Usually we love too little and too sentimentally. Our love, God-given though it be, is usually mixed up with possessiveness and selfishness. It needs strengthening and purifying. Human love is often inordinate, which means disorderly, unregulated, unrestrained, not limited to the usual bounds. If we love someone more than we love God, it is worse than inordinate—it is idolatry. When God is first in our hearts, all other loves are in order and find their rightful place. If God is not first, other loves, even those which are in no sense sexual, easily turn into self-gratification and therefore destroy both the lover and the beloved.

Vanauken had constructed a world for himself and the

woman he loved, and thrown up around it what they called The Shining Barrier. Shutting out all else, they determined to make things work their way. It was a rigid structure, perilously maintained, and when Christ came into their lives it cracked. "Any man who falls on that stone will be dashed to pieces; and if it falls on a man he will be crushed by it" (Luke 20:10, NEB).

Lewis helped Vanauken to see that his very agony was the mercy of God.

In His mercy God stands silently by and permits us to agonize. We simply cannot turn to Him until we have nowhere else to turn. Francis Thompson's poem, "The Hound of Heaven," describes a lonely man's attempt to flee Him and find solace elsewhere.

> I fled Him, down the nights and down the days;
>   I fled Him, down the arches of the years;
> I fled Him, down the labyrinthine ways
>   Of my own mind; and in the mist of tears
> I hid from him ...

He tried romantic love, he tried the love of children, he tried Nature, while

> Still with unhurrying chase,
>   And unperturbed pace,
> Deliberate speed, majestic instancy,
>   Came on the following Feet ...

At last the Hound chases him to earth. He hears a Voice around him, "like a bursting sea," which says:

> "All which I took from thee I did but take,
>   Not for thy harms, but just that thou shouldst
>   seek it in My arms,
> All which thy child's mistake fancies as lost,
>   I have stored for thee at home;
> Rise, clasp My hand, and come!"

"Not for thy harms." Like a skilled surgeon, God may have to hurt us, but He will never harm us. His object is wholeness.

"Stored for us at home." Everything we have lost? Did we only fancy it as lost? How can this be?

We may not ask too many questions about the *hows* of God's secret work. Consider this list of questions:

Can God spread a table in the wilderness?

Has your God been able to save you from the lions?

Can these bones live again?

How is the Lord to save Jerusalem?

Is this your care for the widow?

Which way are we to turn?

Why wait any longer for Him to help us?

Where can we buy bread?

How can a man be born when he is old?

How can you give me living water?

How can this man give us his flesh to eat?

How is it that this untrained man can teach?

What is the good of that for such a crowd?

Who will roll away the stone?[1]

We may add our own burning question about *how* God stores things for us at home. If a child has died, the answer may not seem too difficult—the child is in heaven. But other losses?

The Bible is a book about the mysterious ways of God with individual men. It shows us on every page that there is a Controller. We have a tendency to dismiss the possibility of mystery in our own lives, even when we are faithful readers and professed believers of the Bible, with remarks like, "Oh, but that was back then." Jesus Christ is the same. Yesterday. Today. Forever. We have innumerable promises that the Seen is not the whole story. The Unseen is where it is to be finally unfurled.

"Our troubles are slight and short-lived; and their outcome an eternal glory which outweighs them far. Meanwhile our eyes are fixed, not on the things that are seen, but on the things that are unseen: for what is seen passes away; what is unseen is eternal" (2 Cor. 4:17-18, NEB).

How shall we be sure that the word "not for thy harms" is true? How shall we fix our eyes on things unseen? There is no answer but faith, faith in the character of God Himself. That and no other is the anchor for our souls.

Chapter Ten

Death Is a
New Beginning

My friend Kathy has just married off her second daughter. She has one left at home. Her way of facing the loneliness of the "empty nest" differs radically from the usual. This is what she wrote to me:

> As painful and emotional as it seems *now* that Amy will be at home only one more year, *I know* that *then* there will be grace sufficient and a new set of marching orders. And this gives such hope, for *the Giver of the promise may be trusted!*

The promise Kathy refers to, of course, is God's Word to Paul: "My grace is sufficient for you, for My strength is made perfect in weakness" (2 Cor. 12:19, NKJV). And a new set of marching orders. That is what always follows loss of any kind— a mother's loss of her child, a wife's of her husband, a lover's of his beloved, a man's loss of his job, his health, his self-esteem, his home—if only we have ears to hear those orders, eyes to see the gain God intends to bring out of our loss. Even when trouble stops our ears and clouds our vision, He goes on working in secret and perhaps years later reveals what we had not faith to lay hold of.

"I do not want to miss one lesson," I wrote a few weeks after Jim died.

> Yet I find that events do not change souls. It is our response to them which finally affects us. I find that though I am in a new place of yieldedness before Him who has thus planned my life, little things remain between me and Him— big things in His sight: lack of patience with the Indians, laziness in myself, failure to discipline myself to prepare properly for school [literacy classes which I was teaching Quichua girls], etc.

Two days later:

> Got so impatient with the girls in school that I had to come downstairs for awhile and write a letter just for a break. Then the afternoon held the instruction class for those who teach the children's meeting. I feel helpless without Jim—he always taught that class. A thousand little things come up constantly—gasoline for the lamps—where did he store it? Someone broke into the storeroom—what did they steal? I don't know what was in it. Hector [teacher of the Indian school] came up to discuss his salary—such a complicated business, I don't understand it at all.

I include these entries, samples of many similar ones, to show that although my spiritual ambitions were high, the gift of widowhood certainly did not catapult me into sainthood. I can look back and see that the Spirit of God did not stop His work in me—His work in a soul is often "without observation," a hidden thing like yeast. While I understood that in so great a loss God surely must have some great gain in mind, I was not nearly saintly enough always to see the little needling trials of the day as my "marching orders," the very process itself through which God's great gain would be realized. I was to *march*, not to leap and bound. It was left, right, left, right.

Waking in the morning was always the worst time—*Oh dear, another day without him!* was my thought. Then the Lord's loving reminder, in the words of an old hymn:

Still, still with Thee, when purple morning breaketh,
When the bird waketh, and the shadows flee;
Fairer than morning, lovelier than daylight
Dawns the sweet consciousness, I am with Thee.

Harriet Beecher Stowe

The consciousness of His presence had never before in any special way seemed "lovelier than daylight." Now, because of death, it did.

Death is a new beginning. Lilias Trotter's little gem of a book, *Parables of the Cross*, illustrates this mysterious principle with watercolors of flowers and seed pods. Beside a painting of a calyx which has released all of the petals she writes,

Look at the expression of abandonment about this wild-rose calyx as time goes on, and it begins to grow towards the end for which it has had to count all things but loss: the look of dumb emptiness has gone—it is flung back joyously now, for simultaneously with the new dying a richer life has begun to work at its heart—so much death, so much life—for

"Ever with death it weaveth

The warp and woof of the world."

… The seed-vessel has begun to form; it is "yielded to bring forth fruit."

Deeper and deeper must be the dying, for wider and fuller is the lifetide that it is to liberate—no longer limited by the narrow range of our own being, but with endless powers of multiplying in other souls. Death must reach the very springs of our nature to set it free: it is not this thing or that thing that must go now: it is blindly, helplessly, recklessly, our very selves. A dying must come upon *all* that would hinder God's working through us—all interests, all impulses, all energies that are "born of the flesh"—all that is merely human and apart from His Spirit.[1]

"Deeper and deeper must be the dying." The vocabulary sounds morbid, a word which comes from the Latin for disease, related to the verb "to die." But the spiritual meaning of death which Trotter's book illustrates, far from being a diseased and unwholesome thing, is actually the wondrous matrix of health, well-being, vitality, *life*. Loneliness is one kind of "dying" most of us learn about sooner or later. Far from being "bad" for us, a hindrance to spiritual growth, it may be the means of unfolding spiritual "blossoms" hitherto enfolded. The full-blown beauty of the wild rose, its very "fulfillment," depends on its continuously dying and living again. The death of the seed that falls into the ground produces a new cycle of life—the fresh little shoot, the full stalk, the bud, the flower. The flower must die in order to produce the fruit. The fruit dies to allow the seed to fall once again into the ground. The seed dies and there is a new beginning. Nothing is ever wasted. Dead leaves, dead flesh, natural wastes of all kinds, enrich the soil. In God's economy, whether He is making a flower or a human soul, nothing ever comes to nothing. The losses are His way of accomplishing the gains.

*   *   *

The same Mind which fashioned the cycles of seed life also fashioned the continuous death-and-life cycle of an individual human life. Our lives could not begin without the mother's life-giving. Spanish calls the giving of birth the giving of *light*. Yet this very initiation into life and light is in itself an experience of death—death for the mother, who puts her life on the line to deliver her child, and death for the child, who leaves the security and warmth of the womb to travel a terrible passage into a cold and unfamiliar world.

Every passage is both a death and a new life. When the child is weaned there is the severing from the only source of comfort and nourishment he has known. Suddenly he is *lonely*. So is the mother, as she experiences the first separation from her baby who has been intimately and physically a part of her. Weaning is thus a death for both baby and mother.

When the child learns to walk he walks away from his mother. When he leaves for school it is the end of measureless freedom and the security of home. He finds out what loneliness is, and so does the mother, for even if she feels that for her it is the beginning of a new freedom, she must also realize that she has lost her baby.

Puberty, the foreshadowing of the new life of fatherhood and motherhood, is death to the old one of childhood. Jesus made a break with His parents at the age of twelve to be about His Father's business. The time of irresponsibility was over for Him (Is there a lesson here for teenagers and their parents? How long can playtime go on?). When Amy goes to college, her mother "loses her baby" all over again, as Kathy's letter depicts.

Graduation ceremonies are called commencements. They celebrate both an ending and a beginning. Young adulthood is a new life, eagerly welcomed, yet seldom entered upon without some pangs of nostalgia, not to mention qualms about the future. So it is a death as well. One is jolted by the realization that he is no longer protected and cared for, he is on his own and has obligations he never had before. It dawns on him, for example, that he is single, although he has never been anything else. What does it mean? Death to self-will, a new life of acceptance of suffering, a serious seeking of the will of God concerning marriage.

Nowhere is the life/death cycle more obvious than in marriage. While bride and groom, consumed with joy, may well make it through the wedding without tears, the parents often do not. Newlyweds focus on the new life. Parents focus on the one that is over. It does not take long after the wedding, however, for the young husband and wife to discover that marriage is both a new life and an unexpected death. At this point each is likely to feel that a horrible mistake has been made. Marriage is death to privacy, independence, childhood's home and family, death to unilateral decisions and the notion that there is only one way of doing things, death to the self. When these little deaths are gladly and wholeheartedly accepted, new life—the glory of sacrificial love which leads to perfect union—is inevitable.

Then, in the normal course of things, follows parenthood, fraught with joy and pain. A new life, and a radically new laying down of life begins—through all of the sacrifices and sufferings of birth, weaning, training, school, puberty, adolescence, marriage, each with a different kind of loneliness. Thus the cycle goes on—life out of death, gain out of loss.

This is what the Crucified Life is all about. The Cross is a sign of loss—shameful, humiliating, abject, total loss. Yet it was Jesus' loss that meant heavenly gain for the whole world. Although secured in a tomb with a heavy stone, a seal, and posted guards, He could not be held down by death. He came out of the grave as the Death of Death and Hell's Destruction.

His death was a new beginning. Those who accept that truth receive not only the promise of heaven, but the possibility of heaven on earth, where the Risen Christ walks with us, transforming, if we allow Him to, even an empty nest.

Chapter Eleven

The Price Is Outrageous

It is wintertime as I am writing this. My afternoon walks take me along a shore road lined with wild rosebushes and bittersweet. The bittersweet holds its crusty little orange and yellow pods. The rosebushes are dried brown thickets of wicked thorns and shriveled rosehips. I see in them the stark beauty to which Lilias Trotter opened my eyes—the signs of death, which presage the signs of life.

Using another metaphor in his book, *The Mirror of the Sea*, Joseph Conrad sees death as both a landfall and a departure, an arriving and a leaving, the two things that mark the rhythmical swing of a seaman's life and of a ship's career. Describing his last visit with his old captain who was dying, he writes,

I observed his weary eyes gaze steadily ahead, as if there had been nothing between him and the straight line of sea and sky, where whatever a seaman is looking for is first bound to appear. But I have also seen his eyes rest fondly upon the faces in the room, upon the pictures on the wall, upon all the familiar objects of that home, whose abiding and clear image must have flashed often on his memory in times of stress and anxiety at sea. Was he looking out for a strange Landfall, or taking with an untroubled mind the bearings for his last Departure? It is hard to say, for in that voyage from which no man returns Landfall and Departure are instantaneous, merging together into one moment of supreme and final attention.[1]

Loneliness, as we have noted, is a kind of death. Looking at it through the eyes of the old sea captain, perhaps we may see it as a simultaneous exit and entrance. The loneliness of widowhood was an exit from the comforts and consolations of having a husband, and an entrance into the strange world of having to make unilateral decisions again and to learn to say "I" instead of "we." With the grace of God and the passage of time (also one of His graces), I got used to that world. But that was not the end of God's story. When I fell in love with my present husband, Lars Gren, I was lonely all over again. We were not separated for long years as Jim and I had been, yet I missed him. The house in which I had got used to living alone suddenly seemed empty.

Then we were married. Marriage, too, as we have noted, is a death—a Landfall and Departure, a launching out into unknown deeps for which we need chart and compass. Who knows what is in store for him when he stands, in the wedding ceremony, "before God and these witnesses" and is charged "as ye will answer at the dreadful day of judgment when the secrets of all hearts shall be disclosed"? He makes prodigious promises to "love her, comfort her, honor and keep her in sickness and in health; and, forsaking all others, keep only unto her," so long as they both shall live. Does he know what he is saying when he takes her as his wedded wife, "to have and to hold from this day forward, for better for worse, for richer for poorer, in sickness and in health, to love and to cherish, till death us do part"? What if it turns out not better, richer, and healthier, but worse, poorer, and sicker? Has he a warrant then to abandon his vows? Never. It was for this that he made *vows*, not mere promises. There are no footnotes or conditions attached.

When my beloved Uncle Tom was in his eighties, and had cancer himself, he gave Aunt Dot, his wife, round-the-clock nursing care for four years, the last years of her life. When she died, I told him how greatly I admired his willingness to do this. I said I did not think many men would have done what he did, and I thought he was wonderful.

"Wonderful?" he said. "What's wonderful about it? It's what I promised to do, isn't it?" Bless his great heart!

Who knows what he is getting into when he decides to follow Christ with no turning back? Christ, like the bridegroom, offers everything. The old wedding ceremony (now sadly altered) requires the man to say, "With this ring I thee wed, with my body I thee worship, and with all my worldly goods I thee endow." He is promising everything he is, everything he has. So does God. "All things are yours. ... And you are Christ's, and Christ is God's" (1 Cor. 3:21, 23, NKJV).

Discipleship is exactly like marriage in many ways. In both Old and New Testaments the profoundly intimate relationship between God and His people is represented by the analogy of bridegroom and bride. The prophet Isaiah says to Israel, "Your husband is your maker, whose name is the Lord of Hosts.... The Lord has acknowledged you a wife again ... your God has called you a bride" (Isa. 54:5-6). The apostle Paul uses the marriage relationship to express Christ's love for His Bride, His headship and her submission. In the Book of the Revelation one of the seven angels says to John, "Come, and I will show you the bride, the wife of the Lamb" (Rev. 21:9, NEB). The Book of Common Prayer speaks of matrimony as "an honorable estate, instituted of God, signifying unto us the mystical union that is betwixt Christ and His Church."

Christ has already given us everything when He gave us Himself. He asks for everything in return—there must be no reserved corners, no secret disclaimers, no insistence on individual rights, no escape clauses. The bride, in the old ceremony, promises not only to have, hold, love, and cherish, but also to *obey,* "according to God's holy ordinance." Where do women get the idea they can omit that?

Obedience is a part of love's burden—for the disciple as for the wife.

A disciple is also a soldier. Père Didon, in his *Spiritual Letters,* wrote,

I do not want people who come with me under certain reservations. In battle you need soldiers who fear nothing. The roads are rugged, the precipices are steep; there may be feelings of dizziness on the heights, gusts of wind, peals of thunder, fierce eagles, nights of awful gloom; fear them not! There are also the joys of sunlight, flowers such as are not in the plain, the purest of air, restful nooks, and the stars smile thence like the eyes of God.[2]

Jesus never lured disciples by false advertising. Once, when great crowds were following Him, He turned to them and said, "If anyone comes to me and does not hate his father and mother, wife and children, brothers and sisters, even his own life, he cannot be a disciple of mine. No one who does not carry his cross and come with me can be a disciple of mine" (Luke 14:26-27, NEB).

With terms like that, there was never a stampede to join Him then. There is not likely to be one now. The requirements have not been modernized as the marriage vows have. The requirements for discipleship are very much like the old marriage vows: impossible.

Jesus underlined the impossibility by telling about a man figuring the cost of building a tower, and a king who has an army of ten thousand. "Can he face an enemy coming to meet him with twenty thousand?" asks Jesus.[3] "Which means to say," writes M. Maritain,

before setting to work for God and to fight against the devil, first calculate your forces; and if you consider yourself well enough equipped to begin you are a fool, because the tower to be built costs an outrageous price, and the enemy coming out to meet you is an angel before whom you are of no account. Get to know yourself so well that you cannot contemplate yourself without flinching; then there will be room for hope. Only in the sure knowledge that you are obliged to do the impossible and that you can do the impossible in him who strengthens you are you ready for a task which can be performed only through the cross.[4]

Is Jesus about to make some kind of deal with potential recruits? Will He waive a few of the requisites? No. He adds one more: "So also none of you can be a disciple of mine without parting with all his possessions" (Luke 14:31, NEB).

Marriage is like that too. No bride or groom can enter marriage without surrendering the right to self. But of course people get married all the time with no intention whatever of doing that. In most cases nobody has told them they need to, and their understanding of the nature of love is wildly fanciful. They have found a human being who, they suppose, is capable of meeting their needs—the perfect mate, compatible, lovable, comprehensible. But this prize package is always a surprise package. They are headed for trouble, for unless they learn daily to make the sacrifices of love, the marriage is at best only a "working relationship," not a union. At worst, it dissolves.

Who can possibly enter into marriage, much less discipleship? The Lord asks far too much. Surely He does not expect it of us. Surely He exaggerates.

Does He? Twice He repeats His unequivocal words to

great *crowds.* He is not speaking privately to the twelve whom He had instructed at length in the principles of discipleship, but to the masses. His message is: What I am asking is more than any of you can possibly give. You must ask for terms.

There is no hope for any of us until we confess our helplessness. Then we are in a position to receive grace. There we have the "terms": grace—first, last, and always. So long as we see ourselves as competent we do not qualify. Jesus vividly depicted the obligations as beyond us. But *Come to Me,* He says. *Carry your cross and come with Me. I alone can make you a disciple.*

The disciple should not be surprised if, as he travels the road with Christ, some of the old gang begins to thin out. He may feel lonely at first, but then he sees that there are many Companions of the Way whom he would never have met on a lower road. A college student said to me, "You realize you're talking to a *very* small audience." I asked what he meant. "You're only talking to people who are really *serious* about following Christ. Most of us don't think we have to go that far."

It is heartening to know that there are in fact many who want to go all the way. The letters I get prove it. Here is one from a man who has watched what he believed was a friendship destined to deepen and blossom into marriage wither and crumble to dust.

He told me the story from the beginning, its ups and downs, his heart-searchings and assurances from the Lord, her warm responses and cold shoulders, his patient waiting. He prayed that the Lord would show him what it means to love one's wife as

Christ loved the Church and gave Himself up for her. It seemed that to put his own wants and needs aside in deference to hers was not a hard thing to do, for he loved her. She made it clear that she did not feel for him what he felt for her.

In the heat of emotion it's tough to see straight. To lay my hopes and desires of spending our lives together upon the altar was a dimension I never considered. That was everything! Could God, would God ask for so much? ... I do not know what will come of this sacrifice. I do know that obedience is the question. To that end I have tried to do my best to be faithful. A sacrifice of this type is not a one-time event. It must happen every time I see her, every time I remember her. Sacrifice, obedience, and grace are the instruments of victory here. It is a miracle in the making, a testimony of God's love overcoming despair, brokenness, and self.

My only recourse was to my knees. I prayed for understanding and direction. I believed the Lord was telling me to hang in there. So I did. Every night I would pray for the Lord to continue His healing work in Roxanne [not her real name] and that His character would be manifested in her life. I also prayed that I would be faithful to persevere during that time so that His love would shine in my life. The mystery of the meaning of Christ's sacrifice for the Church was something I needed to know more about, so I asked God to show me how that could be manifested in my life.

Roxanne's attitude changed. There were more freedom, greater warmth, better communication.

I couldn't believe how good those times were! We thoroughly enjoyed each other's company. She was the type of friend I had longed for over many years. I loved to do things with her and for her. Nothing was a burden. It was a joy to serve her and be a support. It was at that time that I wrote to you because I realized that if there were equal feelings on her part I would dishonor my Lord to move ahead without commitment to love and serve her for the rest of my life. In my heart I purposed to do so.

This was followed by difficulties of various kinds. Then she asked that they not see each other so much. Richard [not his real name] agreed, continued to pray for God's work in both hearts. Then she began to feel trapped, became cold and distant, finally told Richard he was a "very special friend," but there was "no romance" in her heart for him.

I am chilled to the very core. How could I have been so wrong? I feel I'm in a void, unable to see and fearful to love. It is very difficult to trust my interpretations of God's word as they might apply to specific circumstances. My sense of vision has been clouded to the point of near blindness. Nonetheless the one ray of light that pierces through this darkness is God's love for me. The house may have been swept away but the foundation is intact.... At this time when I feel so weak and hurt is the opportunity for me to put my faith on the line. To let the love Paul speaks of in Corinthians, and the fruit of the Spirit noted in Galatians, be made profoundly manifest in my life now is to participate in the victory of Christ. It is at this point that I must press on because in that perseverance is the fertile soil where God will plant and nurture the seed of His strength; and it is in His strength that I can live.

Perhaps it seems I have wandered far from the thicket of thorns and shriveled rosehips on the windswept coast, with which I began this chapter. The principle applies—life springs out of death. What rose may spring into flower, perhaps long hence in Richard's life, from this thicket of thorns?

Chapter Twelve

The Intolerable Compliment

When the king of Aram planned to attack Israel, God revealed this to the prophet Elisha, who then warned the king of Israel. Thinking a traitor was responsible for the leak, the king of Aram asked who it might be. One of his staff said, "Don't blame us! Why, you can't even talk in your own bedroom without Elisha the prophet in Israel's knowing what you say!"

"Go and find out where he is," said the king, "and I will seize him" (2 Kgs 6:13, NEB).

Early the next morning Elisha's disciple saw that the city of Dothan was surrounded by horses and chariots.

"Oh, master," he said, "which way are we to turn?"

"Do not be afraid" was Elisha's reply, "for those who are on our side are more than those on theirs."

The prophet had long since learned a lesson which was new to the young man: Invisible forces are always at work. The God who made us does not then leave us to fend for ourselves. He is still Emmanuel, "God *with* us," even when to all appearances we stand alone against frightening forces.

Perhaps you have left home for the first time. I remember how daunting a prospect that was for me as a fourteen-year-old, about to travel a thousand miles by train to boarding school. I was excited until my parents and younger brothers and sister began almost imperceptibly to slide out of my vision as the silver streamliner, the Tamiami Champion, pulled slowly out of the Philadelphia station, bound for Florida. Suddenly there was a great sickening hollow in the middle of my stomach as I realized how very much my family and my home meant to me. I would not see them again for nine long months.

Perhaps you are just starting college, or have moved to a new town where you know no one. You are a stranger and people scrutinize you strangely. You have a new job, new responsibilities you are not sure you can meet. Maybe you have no job at all because you've been fired or are retired. Maybe your situation is that of being the only believer among nonbelievers. Good recipes for loneliness, all of them. For one reason or another you are like Elisha's servant, in a panic, feeling defenseless and alone, wondering which way to turn.

Our faithful heavenly Father knows what a battle it is for us flesh-and-blood creatures to focus on the spiritual. As long as we live in a material world it will be a battle. But He is there to help and cheer us if we'll ask Him to. He will open our eyes to the Unseen if we'll pray for it. Remember Paul's encouragement to the Corinthians, how he reminded them that the outcome of human problems is "a weight of glory," *when* we fix our gaze on things unseen, which will never pass away, rather than on things seen, which will all pass away.

Is it easier to see Elisha's disciple as surrounded by chariots of fire than it is to see ourselves so surrounded? Has God, in our case, forgotten to be gracious? Are we at the mercy of the king of Aram, or have we faith to see what the prophet saw?

Last spring I met a young detective from Belfast who has a particularly lonely job. His work takes him into the most dangerous sections of that torn city, and he was afraid. He knew that a bomb or a gun might go off at any moment and he could be killed or "kneecapped" or disabled in some other way. Being a husband and father, he feared not primarily for himself but for his family. Someone gave him the story of the five missionaries in Ecuador. He told me how he would take that book to bed with him at night, read a little, cry over it, pray, and then reread the passage. He had planned to read a chapter a night, but found himself reading and rereading, crying and praying his way through it. "It gave me courage!" he said, his face shining. "I saw that those men did what they did believing that God was in charge of the outcome. I'm not a missionary, but I'm under the same Lord. If those men could do it, I could too."

Even as I write, I see from my window a baby rabbit dart out from the underbrush, followed by the mother. She chases him in a circle for a minute, so fast it looks as though they forget who is chasing whom. Suddenly they both disappear into the underbrush. A minute later a young woodchuck waddles out, vacuums the grass slowly with his black snout, and waddles back. I scan the slope anxiously for a predatory cat that spends a good deal of his time crouching and creeping along the edges of the rabbits' playground. He is not there. The words I was about to write just before these furry things appeared take on a wider meaning:

"No one of us lives, and equally no one of us dies, for himself alone. If we live, we live for the Lord; and if we die, we die for the Lord. Whether therefore we live or die, we belong to the Lord" (Rom. 14:7-9, NEB).

And are we not of much greater value than many sparrows—or bunnies or woodchucks? The life and death of all of us is in the same Hands. We are always surrounded by the Unseen, among whom are the angels, ministers of fire, explicitly commissioned to guard us. He who keeps us neither slumbers nor sleeps. His love is always awake, always aware, always surrounding and upholding and protecting. If a spear or a bullet finds its target in the flesh of one of His servants, it is not because of inattention on His part. It is because of love.

> If God is Love, He is, by definition, something more than mere kindness. And it appears, from all records, that though He has often rebuked us and condemned us, He has never regarded us with contempt. He has paid us the intolerable compliment of loving in the deepest, most tragic, most inexorable sense.[1]

Whether we live or die, we belong to the Lord. Live each hour of each day *with Him as Lord,* for "this is why Christ died and came to life again, to establish his lordship over dead and living" (Rom. 14:9, NEB).

If His lordship is really established over me, it makes no difference (I might even say it's "no big deal") whether I live or die. I am expendable. That knowledge is freedom. I have no care for anything, for all that I am, all that I have, all that I do, and all that I suffer have been joyfully placed at His disposal. He can do anything He wants.

What do we think He wants? Gerard Manley Hopkins expressed the answer most beautifully in "The Golden Echo":

> See; not a hair is, not an eyelash, not the least
>   last lost; every hair
> Is, hair of the head, numbered.
> Nay, what we had lighthanded left in surly
>   the mere mould
> Will have waked and have waxed and have walked
>   with the wind what while we slept,
> This side, that side hurling a heavyhearted hundredfold
> What while we, while we slumbered.
> O then, weary then why should we tread? O why are
>   we so haggard at the heart, so care-coiled,
>   care-killed, so fagged, so fashed, so cogged,
>   so cumbered,
> When the thing we freely forfeit is kept with fonder
>   a care,
> Fonder a care kept than we could have kept it, kept
> Far with fonder a care (and we, we should have lost
>   it) finer, fonder
> A care kept.—Where kept? Do but tell us where kept,
>   where.—
> Yonder.—What high as that! We follow, now we follow.—
>   Yonder, yes yonder, yonder,
> Yonder.[2]

Chapter Thirteen

Married but Alone

If I try to write for all who experience aloneness in any form, I tread often on unfamiliar ground. I have not been there, and I cannot say, "I understand perfectly. I know exactly what you are going through." In various wildernesses, I have found the companionship of Him who is "no High Priest who cannot sympathize with our weaknesses—he himself has shared fully in all our experience of temptation, except that he never sinned" (Heb. 4:15, PHILLIPS).Think of it: Every one of our human weaknesses is intelligible to Him. He understands. He shares fully.

To be a disciple of Jesus Christ is to have a Companion all the time. But that does not mean we will never suffer loneliness. In fact, it means that we may be lonely in ways we would not have been if we had not chosen to be disciples. When people who are contemplating becoming missionaries ask me, "But what about loneliness?" I tell them, Yes. You'll be lonely. It's part of the price. Strangers in strange lands are lonely. You accept that in advance.

As in discipleship, so in marriage. One of the surprises in store for most brides and grooms is that they are still lonely. A common but unreasonable expectation about marriage (and there are many unreasonable ones) is that the partner will now fill the place of everybody on whom one depended before— father, mother, brothers, sisters, friends. Because "falling in love" is an all-consuming, preoccupying, and exclusive phenomenon, it can be very hard on other relationships which no longer seem to be needed. But marriage teaches us that even the most intimate human companionship cannot satisfy the deepest places of the heart. Our hearts are lonely till they rest in Him who made us for Himself.

In a question-and-answer session at a women's conference I was asked, What would you say to a daughter who is about to divorce her husband because he isn't meeting all her needs? There was a ripple of laughter from the audience. The folly of such a demand! I said I would try to point out to the poor girl that she is asking of her husband what no human being can ask of anybody. Having been married to three very different men, all of them fine Christian husbands, I have found that no one of them, or even all three of them together if I had been a polyandrist, could "meet all my needs." The Bible promises me that my God, not my husband, shall supply all my needs.

Writes Paul Tillich, "Man and woman remain alone even in the most intimate union. They cannot penetrate each other's innermost center. And if this were not so they could not be helpers to each other; they could not have human community."[1]

Failure in communication, according to a recent poll, is the number one cause of divorce. Recently the exuberant and blunt Oprah Winfrey was questioning people on what went wrong in marriage.

"If I hear that word communication ONE—MORE—TIME—," she said, rolling her eyes. Then she turned to the "expert" (which usually means anybody who has written a book on anything) and asked what communication means.

"It doesn't MEAN A THING!" was his answer.

"Thank you," said Oprah.

So much for that. But one way or another, we must get through to people occasionally, and we all fail in that sometimes, not only with spouses but with others. We don't take the time to write the letter, make the phone call, visit, sit down and listen. If we are hungry to talk to someone about something we can't always find anyone who will listen. Some people are gifted communicators, but most of us, gifted or not, could do better. Given the ontological difference which Tillich describes, plus differences in personalities, background, education, language, and interests, communication can never be perfect, but it is not unreasonable to ask for improvement in this area.

Jim, Add, and Lars (my husbands, in that order) have differed in ability, and I have had to learn to be realistic and reasonable in my expectations. Add, who was a very popular speaker and the author of eight books, was, in my opinion, a communicator of the first water. His love letters during our courtship were such masterpieces that I have actually considered publishing them (and thought better of it) as *Love Letters of a Theologian*. What he thought and felt about me he knew how to put into words.

He did not stop doing that when I became his wife, but I found him strangely reticent to speak of many things which profoundly affected his life.

To find someone who "reads" us, responds wholeheartedly to us, and with real understanding, is a rare gift. Many people find themselves married to partners who are on a totally different intellectual or spiritual wavelength, as Ruth Sanford describes in her book, *Do You Feel Alone in the Spirit?*[2] I gather from the number of women who speak to me about this kind of loneliness and isolation that it is a common one.

One gets the impression that most husbands now are caught up in their work at least five days a week, and when they come home want only to "relax," which does not mean sitting down and talking with wives and children, but turning on the television, picking up the newspaper, or going to the health club. I suppose the same could be said of some working wives. If both work, it is hard to imagine how they will manage even to be friends. Each expects the other to be available when wanted. If the other isn't, the loneliness that results is hard to take.

A woman whom I'll call Priscilla told me of an experience of loneliness in marriage unlike any I had heard of. Her husband, who is a professing Christian and seemed in a casual meeting a decent sort, has turned out to be quite uncivilized and quite unchristian. Although they live together as husband and wife (she says he can be wonderfully loving and appreciative), he has in a very strange way abandoned her. He appears to have made a decision before they were married (of which he told her nothing) that she would pay all the bills. When this became apparent after the honeymoon, the only explanation he offered was that she has a good job, she was doing very well before she married him, it doesn't cost much for him to live in her comfortable condominium and eat at her table—why shouldn't she foot the bills? Poor woman. Thinking she had married a husband, she finds she has married a nonpaying guest. She's isolated. She's shocked, baffled, lonely.

"Why am I in this?" she asked me. It echoes the cry of so many. We were sitting by the fire in her beautifully decorated living room. We had just finished an excellent dinner which she had cooked. As always, she was elegantly dressed. I was thinking how fortunate her husband is to possess such a woman—pleasant, gentle, sweet-spirited, thoroughly feminine, a real homemaker who also holds a high-paying job. How could he treat her in the ways she described? Of course I know only a fraction of the story, her version. What would his be?

I did not know what to say. The question of what to *do* with a husband like that I could not answer. I had never been in her shoes, but I had certainly asked the more fundamental question in situations which had nothing to do with marriage: *Why am I in this?* Sometimes the answer included mistakes of my own, sometimes those of others, sometimes nobody's.

This is not a book on marital counseling. There is no shortage of those. We are here attempting to face the ultimate questions, such as the one Priscilla asked. There may be many things she can do as time goes by, but before any hint of a change takes place in her situation or her husband, she can go directly to God. He knows why she is in this.

The ultimate answer goes to the Origin of things. Why am I widowed? Why has God allowed a divorce? Why hasn't He given me a wife (or a husband)? Why do my friends misunderstand me? Why would God give me a husband who doesn't accept responsibility? Why can't we communicate? Why did I lose the person who meant most to me in all the world? Why should I, why should anybody be all alone?

Where there are no answers in the present, my mind insists on pushing the questions as far back as possible. Everything that comes up has something to do with *God*. It is meant to bring me face to face with Him and to teach me something about His ways with us. How far back can we push this question of loneliness? Is Priscilla's or yours or mine the result of circumstances or people we can't control? Is anybody in control? Are we all adrift in nothingness or is there someone in charge of the whole scene?

Science is always explaining causes and effects, but to the question of the Original Cause—how did the universe begin?—science gives us strange answers. The explosion theory is one of them. The scientist can tell us exactly why an explosion occurs, whether by choice in a laboratory or by accident in or out of a laboratory. It is the result of the sudden production of great pressure. In other words, it is *caused*. We can count on that. *Something* made it happen. Everything, including the universe itself, they tell us, is caused. That's what science is about. The idea of a Primary Cause, however, is usually ruled out—because, as one scientist stated, "to the scientific mind it is simply intolerable." Science is content to say that matter produced mind. It refuses to entertain the possibility that Mind produced matter.[3]

But this original Big Bang—are we to believe that it alone, among all explosions, was *not* preceded by the sudden production of pressure? Was there no cause at all? Wrong question, we are told. Irrelevant. Unnecessary. It happened. There comes a point where you stop asking about causes. The notion of an Originator is not susceptible to laboratory testing.

Perhaps we can stop with that so long as our thinking is merely theoretical. It's when things personal occur that the question breaks out most insistently. As Kierkegaard said about Hegelianism, the science of his day: "Hegel explained everything in the universe except what it is to be an individual, to be born, to live, and to die."[4]

When I sit on Priscilla's sofa and look at the pain in her eyes I am thrown back again to the prior questions. What is it to be an individual, to be born, to live, to die? What does it all mean? Priscilla's husband is the immediate cause of the pain. She has tried talking to him. She has done her very best to make him see what he is doing to her. She has pleaded with him to be a man. But if she cannot change him (and of course she cannot), is she at his mercy or is there another Mercy to appeal to?

Dr. Cressy Morrison, president of the New York Academy of Sciences back in the 1930s, once gave a talk on the Law of Chance. If you take ten pennies and mark them with numbers one through ten and put them in your pocket, he said, your chances of pulling out Number One first would, of course, be one in ten. Your chances of pulling out all the pennies in numerical order would be one in ten billion. He then raised the question of what would be the chances of the universe having just "happened," that life sprang spontaneously from utter lifelessness, that the prodigious intricacies of the human mind originated in mindlessness, that Something came from absolutely Nothing.

The odds against all that would be incalculable, Dr. Morrison said. But he happened to be a Christian. He believed in God.

So does Priscilla, yet she felt as though she were helplessly sinking into an abyss. Had God forgotten to be gracious? Had He in anger shut up His tender mercies?

Why am I in this?

Is it for nothing? Or is it for something?

Months have gone by since that evening by the fire. Friends and family have urged Priscilla to get rid of this man. Divorce is the obvious answer, but it is not an answer she will accept. She has been through one of those and knows she does not want another. Human reason would conclude that a separation at least is the only possible course. Yet—and here is the point—she writes of the presence of God, of a deep heart-desire to learn of Him in the midst of it all, of a determination to fulfill her vows at any cost. Who can say that she is mistaken? Who knows the gains which may come of her daily losses?

Her latest letter, depicting an even worse scenario, ends with:

But the Lord has been so *faithful*. In agony I have lain prostrate before Him and "wailed." I had to have chosen the wrong one. He so graciously gave me His word in John 6:70, "Did I not *choose* the Twelve of you myself? Yet one of you is a devil." And so He has assured me that even in our finite poor judgment in choosing, I know He has gone before.

Words written to people in trouble many centuries ago by a man who knew a great deal of trouble at firsthand show that there is another level on which the happenings in our lives may be understood:

In my opinion whatever we may have to go through now is less than nothing compared with the magnificent future God has in store for us. The whole creation is on tiptoe to see the wonderful sight of the sons of God coming into their own. The world of creation cannot as yet see reality, not because it chooses to be blind, but because in God's purpose it has been so limited—yet it has been given hope. And the hope is that in the end the whole of created life will be rescued from the tyranny of change and decay, and have its share in that magnificent liberty which can only belong to the children of God!

ROMANS 8:18-21, PHILLIPS

There is a future and a plan. There is another reality. This is Priscilla's hope. It is what makes her see things so differently from those who would advise a different course. I cannot say that she is right or wrong, but I am sure God honors an obedient faith. He too walked this lonesome valley. He bore our griefs, carried our sorrows, and died.

It is he who heals the broken in spirit and binds up their wounds, he who numbers the stars one by one and names them one and all.... The Lord gives new heart to the humble and brings evildoers down to the dust. He veils the sky in clouds and prepares rain for the earth; he clothes the hills with grass.... He gives cattle their food.... His pleasure is in those who fear him, who wait for his true love.

PSALM 147:3-4, 6, 8-9, NEB

Chapter Fourteen

Love Means Acceptance

One aspect of the pain of being alone is probing for explanations as to how I managed to "deserve" this when I've tried so hard to be good. We look at friends who seem to have everything who aren't really much "gooder" than we are. Some of them (if we do say so ourselves!) are much worse.

In Job's day it was understood that good would always be the reward for righteousness, and evil would be the punishment for unrighteousness. When "that righteous man" was stripped of houses, crops, animals, servants, sons, daughters, the confidence of his wife, and his own health, there was, so far as his friends could see, only one possible explanation: Job was at fault. Neither they nor he knew of the strange drama enacted in the court of heaven when God called Satan's attention to Job's blameless faithfulness.

"Of course Job trusts you—so far!" was Satan's retort. "You've given him everything. But take it all away and he'll curse you to your face."[1]

We do not know how many times God and Satan have faced each other over a single individual's faithfulness, but we do know that God permits evil to touch everybody, the holiest as well as the wickedest. Satan's question remains: Will he keep on trusting? I can imagine the hosts of heaven (and perhaps of hell) waiting for the answer with bated breath.

The answer of faith is YES. Acceptance. Job on his ash heap does not strike me as a very patient man. He was quickly fed up with his friends and had many questions, arguments, and accusations against God. God let him dish them all out before He began not to answer but to bury Job with an avalanche of unanswerable questions of His own. At last Job acknowledged God's omnipotence and the limitations of his own understanding. "I knew of you only secondhand. Now I see you with my own eyes. Therefore I melt away and repent in dust and ashes." He had nothing left to say.[2]

The faith of Job is astounding in view of how much less he knew of the love of God than we who know Him through the life and death of Jesus Christ. We have a whole Bible full of revelations about suffering. Job's response was perhaps closer to capitulation than acceptance, but it was enough. God told his friends Job had spoken the truth about Him while they had not.

We have been shown the way of acceptance on every page of the life of Jesus. It sprang from love and from trust. He set His face like a flint toward Jerusalem. He took up the Cross of His own will. No one could take His life from Him. He deliberately laid it down. He calls us to take up our crosses. That is a different thing from capitulation or resignation. It is a glad and voluntary YES to the conditions we meet on our journey with Him, because these are the conditions He wants us to share with Him. Events are the *sacraments* of the Will of God—that is, they are visible signs of an invisible Reality. These provide the very place where we may learn to love and trust. Heaven waits for our response.

Accept your share of the hardship that faithfulness to the gospel entails in the strength that God gives you. For he has saved us from all that is evil and called us to a life of holiness— not because of any of our achievements but for his own purpose. Before time began he planned to give us in Christ Jesus the grace to achieve this purpose.

2 TIMOTHY 1:8-10, PHILLIPS

That is a wonderfully comforting word to me. God had included the hardships of my life (which I confess have been *few*) in His original plan. Nothing takes Him by surprise. But nothing is for nothing, either. His plan is to make me holy, and hardship is indispensable for that as long as we live in this hard old world. All I have to do is accept it.

"The life of a soul is so great a thing, that one of those distilled acts of faith and acceptance, without any light or feeling, is of greater activity and of greater vitality in God's sight than the tramp of armies and the power of those who command them."[3]

It is important to repeat that this acceptance I speak of is not passivism, Quietism, fatalism, or resignation. It is not capitulation to evil, or a refusal to do what can and ought to be done to change things. It is a distilled *act* of faith, a laying one's will alongside God's, a putting of oneself at one with His kingdom and His will.

Acceptance is abandonment, the great risk of great lovers, when an awesome power is given over—the power to hurt. No one in the world has such power to hurt as a husband, wife, or intimate friend. To love is to be vulnerable to that power which lies in the hands of the one loved. When a mother looks into the face of her tiny newborn child, she knows that that little creature already has the power to rake her soul with pain, a power which will grow as the child grows. "A sword shall pierce thy own soul," said old Simeon to Mary (Luke 2:35, KJV). To love means to open ourselves to suffering. Shall we shut our doors to love, then, and be "safe"?

Acceptance of discipleship is the utter abandonment of the disciple, the surrender of all rights, to the Master. This abandonment, in all cases, will mean pain. Christ listed some of the troubles His followers could expect, so that they would not be taken by surprise and thus discard their faith in Him. He did not offer immunity. He asked for trust.

Some couples refuse the risk of abandonment and draw up marriage contracts, hoping to shield themselves from the difficulties marriage inevitably brings. Such a contract is self-defeating, for a marriage must be based on trust. A contract presupposes the absence of trust and resorts to the language of politics (equality, rights, fairness) instead of the language of love. Love accepts—*this* man or woman, with all his or her faults, peculiarities, and exigencies. Where there is no trust, no abandonment, no self-giving—in short no such thing as love as the Bible defines it—it is not to be wondered at that such marriages easily collapse.

As we have noted, Jesus published no false advertising. He was offering the kingdom of heaven—bliss, eternal life, fullness of joy. But He spoke of the small gate and the narrow road. He promised suffering, not escape from suffering. You cannot take up a cross and at the same time not take up a cross, or learn how to die and how not to die.

While the Lord draws up no contract with us, the great thing for us is to remember how the kingdom of heaven works—life out of death is the operative principle. Where there is a clear and shining Purpose behind and under and above it all, faith can say an honest YES.

Amy Carmichael knew a good deal about suffering of many kinds, including loneliness. She knew the temptation to try to escape by forgetting, by drowning the trouble with activity, by shutting oneself off from the world, by surrendering to defeat and sullen resentment. She also knew that none of the above would lead to peace. She found what does lead to peace, here and now:

He said, "I will forget the dying faces;
The empty places,
They shall be filled again.
O voices moaning deep within me, cease."
But vain the word; vain, vain:
Not in forgetting lieth peace.

He said, "I will crowd action upon action,
The strife of faction
Shall stir me and sustain;
O tears that drown the fire of manhood, cease."
But vain the word; vain, vain:
Not in endeavor lieth peace.

He said, "I will withdraw me and be quiet,
Why meddle in life's riot?
Shut be my door to pain.
Desire, thou dost befool me, thou shalt cease."
But vain the word; vain, vain:
Not in aloofness lieth peace.

He said, "I will submit; I am defeated.
God hath depleted
My life of its rich gain.
O futile murmurings, why will ye not cease?"
But vain the word; vain, vain:
Not in submission lieth peace.

He said, "I will accept the breaking sorrow
Which God tomorrow
Will to His son explain."
Then did the turmoil deep within him cease.
Not vain the word, not vain;
For in Acceptance lieth peace.[4]

Chapter Fifteen

A Field With a Treasure in It

When Jim Elliot was preparing for missionary work, he saw parallels between the demands of the life to which he believed God was calling him and life in the Yukon a century ago. For both, the prize was gold, although of greatly differing durability. He copied into his journal a part of Robert Service's poem, "The Law of the Yukon":

> Send not your foolish and feeble; send me your strong
> and your sane,
> Strong for the red-rage of battle, sane for I harry them sore.
> Send me men girt for the combat, men who are grit to
> the core...
> And I wait for the men who will win me—and I will not
> be won in a day,
> And I will not be won by weaklings, subtle and suave
> and mild,

But by men with the hearts of Vikings and the simple faith
    of a child,
Desperate, strong, and resistless, unthrottled by
    fear or defeat,
Them will I gild with my treasure, them will I glut
    with my meat.[1]

The old prospectors had to believe that the gold was there. The journey to get it would be torture, but they chose the torture because of the hope. Jim believed there was treasure better than the Yukon's gold, worth any risk, any sacrifice. I think I can picture him now, looking back from the Celestial City to the journey he had made, thinking the price, after all, didn't amount to much.

You and I are not rushing off to the Yukon to dig for gold, any more than Jim was. We are not gluttons for punishment. We are not legendary heroes or heroines. We are only ordinary folks who get out of very comfortable beds in the morning, brush our teeth with running water, put on whatever we like to wear, and eat whatever we want for breakfast. Our lives generally don't seem to call for much courage. We are so accustomed to luxury we think of traffic jams as hardship. It ruins our day if the air conditioner quits, or the waiter says they're fresh out of cherry cheesecake. Of course it is only a matter of time before the traffic jam is unsnarled; time and money can fix the air conditioner; we can order a different dessert. We expect to get things fixed—fast. When we can't, we are at a loss.

Loneliness is much worse than being stuck in a traffic jam or having to do without cheesecake. Perhaps we hardly think of its calling for courage, because we hardly think of it as real suffering, yet it fits the simplest definition I know: having what you don't want, or wanting what you don't have. Loneliness we don't want. It comes from wanting what we don't have.

Who can compare sufferings? They are unique as each sufferer is unique. "The heart knows its own bitterness" (Prov. 14:10, NEB). We respond according to our temperaments. Some cast about for solutions, stew, fret, rage, deny the facts. Some sink into an oblivion of self-recrimination or pity. Some chalk it all up to somebody else's fault. Some pray. But all of us may be tempted sometime to conclude that because God doesn't fix it He doesn't love us.

There are many things that God does not fix precisely *because He loves us.* Instead of extracting us from the problem, He calls us. In our sorrow or loneliness or pain He calls—"This is a necessary part of the journey. Even if it is the roughest part, it is only a part, and it will not last the whole long way. Remember where I am leading you. Remember what you will find at the end—a home and a haven and a heaven."

Courage for the rugged part comes with looking ahead—as the prospectors did in Gold Rush days. The heroes of the world's great legends let themselves in for all kinds of fearsome troubles because of the promise of a great reward—the favor of the king, a pot of gold, marriage to a princess. Because there was a shining goal, they entered in with heart and will to participate in the as-yet unseen and unknown hazards of the dreadful journey. Their heroism lay in acceptance—a wholehearted acceptance of conditions other men would avoid at all cost—and in endurance. The dark caves, tunnels, and labyrinths were not problems to be solved but hazards to be traversed, the storms and heavy seas were to be braved, the giants and monsters to be slain. All were accepted and endured *in view of the prize.*

It is possible both to accept and to endure loneliness without bitterness when there is a vision of glory beyond. This is a very different thing from the sigh of resignation or defeat, the hopeless abandonment to a malevolent fate which merely "sits there and takes it." In circumstances for which there is no final answer in the world, we have two choices: accept them as God's wise and loving choice for our blessing (this is called faith), or resent them as proof of His indifference, His carelessness, even His nonexistence (this is unbelief).

Finding fault with God is sharp temptation, especially when there is no one else to blame. Yielding to that temptation leads to spiritual emptiness.

"Listen to the word of the Lord," wrote the prophet Jeremiah. "What fault did your forefathers find in me, that they wandered far from me, pursuing empty phantoms and themselves becoming empty?" (Jer. 2:4-5, NEB). Who of us has not known a deep and pervading sense of hollowness, as though life has lost its content? Isn't its cause often our having found fault with God?

A few days ago I returned home from a visit with my daughter and her family. There was a sense of loneliness, the cause of which, so far as I can see now, cannot be remedied. I live on the East Coast. Valerie lives on the West. I can never invite my grandchildren over for the night. I can never have the family for

Sunday dinner—and Sunday dinners with my grandparents are among my treasured childhood memories. I can't simply pop into the house in El Toro now and then for a cup of tea. I was tempted to have a Pity Party for myself. Why should I be denied the tremendous blessing and pleasure of being near those dear little children, the people I love most in the world? God could "fix it" if He wanted to. To pursue that line of thought would have put me in the Slough of Despond.

Our loneliness cannot always be fixed, but it can always be accepted as the very will of God for now, and that turns it into something beautiful. Perhaps it is like the field wherein lies the valuable treasure. We must *buy the field*. It is no sun-drenched meadow embroidered with wildflowers. It is a bleak and empty place, but once we know it contains a jewel the whole picture changes. The empty scrap of forgotten land suddenly teems with possibilities. Here is something we can not only accept, but something worth selling everything to buy. In my case, "selling everything" meant giving up the self-pity and the bitter questions. I do not mean we are to go out looking for chances to be as lonely as possible. I am talking about acceptance of the inevitable. And when, through a willed act we receive this thing we did not want, then Loneliness, the name of the field nobody wants, is transformed into a place of hidden treasure.

* * *

The Captain of our Salvation was made perfect through the things which He suffered. I wonder what sort of child He was. I have often wished we knew something of His early years, but the Holy Spirit chose to leave them out of the record. His child-hood, His adolescence, and His young manhood are all hidden from our curiosity. Was it only the three years of public life that prepared Jesus for the Cross, or were the thirty silent years just as necessary? Surely they were essential—the tears and smiles of a baby, the loneliness of His weaning, a child's bewilderment at His parents' refusals, the uncertainties and loneliness of a teen-ager, the unfulfilled desires of a very vigorous and passionate young man. Were they not, in a manner of speaking, a part of the field where for Him the pearl lay?

If the village house in Nazareth which they show tourists nowadays is anything like the one where the little boy Jesus lived, it was not much to speak of, by comparison with the ivory palaces He had left. He at whose word creation sprang into being was subject to the word of His mother Mary. He whose hands had made the worlds learned obedience in a dusty car-penter shop. When Joseph showed Him how to use a tool, did he hold the little hands in his and say, "Like this. Hold it this way"? The boy had to *learn*. He did not make tables and benches by divine fiat. He made them with tools held in human hands. He had to *learn* the skills, learn to be thorough, dependable, prompt, faithful. If He was ever tempted to cut corners, He did not yield to the temptation. He did nothing sloppily. He worked carefully, thoroughly, dependably, promptly, faithfully. Surely He was gracious with the cus-tomers. He *grew* "in favor with God and man" (Luke 2:52, NKJV). The cheerful acceptance of humble work, the small testings of any boy's home life were a part of His preparation for the great testings of His public years, a part of the road which led Him to the Cross.

The headmistress of the boarding school I attended used to say, "Don't go around with a Bible under your arm if you don't sweep under the bed." She was looking for a genuine faith, which is always a practical faith. She wanted no spiritual talk coming out of a messy room. The dust under the bed spoke louder than any pious "testimony."

"The King of Glory rewards His servants not according to the dignity of their office, but according to the love and humility with which they carry it out."[2]

During Jesus' three years as an itinerant rabbi He knew what it was to be weary, hungry, and homeless. The common people heard Him gladly but the religious elite could not stand Him. He was misquoted, misjudged, misrepresented, misunderstood. The Hebrew scholars were forever laying traps for Him, challenging, quarreling, quibbling. He was praised and scorned, followed and forsaken, loved and hated, listened to and rejected, crowned and crucified. He had every reason to feel lonely in the world of men, but it was thus that He "learned" and demonstrated for us the meaning of obedience—through the things that He suffered.

If all He is asking of us just now is the willingness to accept the relatively small discipline of loneliness, can we not see it as a part of His gift of allowing us to walk with Him?

To walk with Him is to walk the Way of the Cross. If the cross we are asked to take up is not presented to us in the form of martyrdom, heroic action of some kind, dragons or labyrinths or even "ministry"—at least something that looks spiritual—are we to conclude that He has waived the requirement?

He never waives the requirement.

There is a pot of gold, there is a king's reward, but it comes at the end of the journey. Yet all along the way there are countless joys if only we will taste and see that the Lord is good. Samuel Rutherford, persecuted for many years because of his obedience to the truth as he understood it, wrote letters filled with expressions of the sweetness of his trials and the loveliness of Christ. He knew the dark side of the Cross, yet could write to Hugh Mackail in 1636,

> Believe me, brother, I give it to you under mine own handwrit, that whoso looketh to the white side of Christ's cross, and can take it up handsomely with faith and courage, shall find it such a burden as sails are to a ship or wings to a bird. I find that my Lord hath overgilded that black tree, and hath perfumed it, and oiled it with joy and gladness.[3]

Thousands upon thousands (I am one of them) have found it so.

Chapter Sixteen

Make Me a Cake

When Maria von Trapp was a young woman she loved the mountains of her native Austria. She thrilled to think that God had given her those mountains as a gift to enjoy.

"If God has given me all of this," she said, "what can I give Him?"

Thinking over what she had to give she saw how paltry it all was. She knew that she must give everything, which to her meant giving her life in a most literal way—going into a convent, becoming a nun, and never coming out. As many disciples discover, the will of God turns out to be quite different from their expectations. Maria went into the convent, but was soon sent out again to become governess to a widower's children. Thence began the story of *The Sound of Music*, familiar to thousands.

To give God everything must mean that I give Him not only my body as a living sacrifice but everything else as well: all that I am, all that I have, all that I do, and all that I suffer. That covers a lot of territory, but the particular ground we are discussing is one form of suffering: loneliness. I have said that it can be seen as a gift—something received and accepted. A gift may also be something offered.

Maria von Trapp began by offering to God the gift of herself. We must begin there too. We do not thereby "enrich" the Lord for, as the old prayer says, "All things come of Thee, O Lord, and of Thine own have we given Thee." We have nothing but what was His in the first place.

"With eyes wide open to the mercies of God, I beg you ... as an act of intelligent worship, to give him your bodies, as a living sacrifice, consecrated to him and acceptable by him" (Rom. 12:1, PHILLIPS).

Here is the place to start. In His wisdom and lovingkindness He gave each of us a particular body, of His design and construction, prepared for us, bearing His image, yet distinct from all others. We cannot offer it unless we first "receive," that is, accept it—with its beauties, its imperfections, its limitations, its potentialities. This body and nobody else's is my offering. It is not, however, mere blood, bone, and tissue. It is the dwelling of the "self"—spirit, mind, heart, will, emotions, temperament. It must be offered wholeheartedly, in simplicity, with no quibbles about its fitness. It is *holy* as the vessels of the tabernacle (pots, shovels, firepans, snuffers, and all the rest, commonplace as they might be) were holy—*because they were offered* (consecrated and set apart) for that service.

All offerings made to God matter to Him because of the single, unique offering of Christ for us. We unite ourselves with

Him in this—we are actually "crucified with" Christ. Then this body, which is the dwelling of myself, becomes the dwelling of God Himself—a temple of the Holy Spirit. It is not my own. It is *acceptable* to God because I am one with Christ and my offering is taken up into His offering.

The love of God in accepting such an offering is like the love of a father whose little child gives him a present bought with money the father gave him. It is a very tender, sympathetic love. It recognizes that the child's loving gift comes out of his utter poverty. The father, who has already given everything ("My dear son, you have been with me all the time and everything I have is yours" [Luke 15:31, PHILLIPS], gives something more in order that his child may have something to give.

Having presented our bodies, is there anything else we may give? The answer is yes, there is everything else—everything God has given us. When the people of God present their gifts to Him in church—music, prayers, money, bread, and wine—they present only what has been given by His gracious bounty. And again they present *themselves* under these tokens, for only the gift made by self-giving love can be offered. Here we enter into the great mystery of the Bread and Wine. Christ has gone before us, giving Himself: *This is My body; this is My blood.* We love because He first loved us. We offer ourselves because He first offered Himself, each saying to the other, My life for yours. The great mystery of the Bread and Wine is Christ offering Himself in love to us and for us—"My life for yours."

It is important to understand very clearly that we have nothing at all to add to the complete sacrifice of Christ which is our very salvation. His offering was perfect. It lacked nothing. Nor is there any need for the old order of sacrifices (the blood of lambs and bulls and all the rest), for Christ establishes "a new order of obedience to the will of God, and in that will we have been made holy by the single unique offering of the body of Jesus Christ.... By virtue of that one offering he has perfected for all time every one whom he makes holy" (Heb. 10:9-10, 14-15, PHILLIPS).

And so He allows us to come. And so He receives our offerings, given by virtue of something He gave us when He made us: freedom of choice, that we might freely choose to love Him and to give ourselves to Him.

No wonder Paul said, "What do you possess that was not given you?" (1 Cor. 4:7, NEB).

Having given my all, I may specifically offer my time, my work, my prayers, my possessions,[1] my praise, and—yes—my sufferings. It is in this mysterious sense that I see loneliness as a gift: It is not only something to be accepted, but something to be offered, as Matheson gave not only the life he owed, but the unsatisfied desire of his heart.

Is it not legitimate, then, to think of loneliness as material for sacrifice? What I lay on the altar of consecration is nothing more and nothing less than what I *have* at this moment, whatever I find in my life now of work and prayer, joys and sufferings.

Some people see singleness as a liability, a handicap, a deprivation, even a curse. Others see it as a huge asset, a license to be a "swinger," an opportunity to do what feels good. I see it as a gift. To make that gift an offering may be the most costly thing one can do, for it means the laying down of a cherished dream of what one wanted to be, and the acceptance of what one did not want to be. *How changed are my ambitions!* the apostle Paul may have thought, for he wrote, "Now I long to know Christ" (Phil. 3:10, PHILLIPS).

During the months of my second husband's terminal illness I sometimes felt I could not bear one more day of seeing him suffer, or one more visit to the doctor who would tell us terrible things that must be done next—things like removing the lower jaw because of the lip cancer, or castration because of the prostate cancer. Everything in me said NO NO NO NO. Add's suffering became mine. The wee hours were filled with nightmarish images of things far worse than death, and I was afraid. What to do?

The answer came to me.

"Offer it up."

My eyes had been opened to this possibility through the reading of Evelyn Underhill's classic, *The Mystery of Sacrifice.* I had never before been taught the deep truth of making all of life an oblation, but this little book had come into my hands just three months before we discovered my husband's illness. I do not know what I would have done without it.

Offer up *what?* I felt like the destitute widow of Zarephath, about to use the last of the flour and oil which stood between her son's and her own starvation, when along came Elijah and told her to bake him a cake first. Because it was the word of the Lord, she obeyed. The effects of that obedience went far beyond her imagination. "There was food for him and for her

and her family for a long time. The jar of flour did not give out
nor did the flask of oil fail, as the word of the Lord foretold
through Elijah" (1 Kings 17:15-16, NEB).

It was only a vaguely remembered fragment of a poem by
Amy Carmichael that brought to mind the analogy between
suffering and the poverty of the widow of Zarephath. I give it
here in full:

Nothing in the House

Thy servant, Lord, hath nothing in the house,
Not even one small pot of common oil;
For he who never cometh but to spoil
Hath raided my poor house again, again,
That ruthless strong man armed, whom men call Pain.

I thought that I had courage in the house,
And patience to be quiet and endure,
And sometimes happy songs; now I am sure
Thy servant truly hath not anything,
And see, my song-bird hath a broken wing.

* * *

My servant, I have come into the house—
I who know Pain's extremity so well
That there can never be the need to tell
His power to make the flesh and spirit quail:
Have I not felt the scourge, the thorn, the nail?

And I, his Conqueror, am in the house,
Let not your heart be troubled: do not fear:

Why shouldst thou, child of Mine, if I am here?
My touch will heal thy song-bird's broken wing,
And he shall have a braver song to sing.[2]

I had nothing in the house. Nothing except this pain. Pain—an offering? What could the Lord possibly make of that?

"Make me a cake." In other words, Elijah said: There *is* one thing you can do. Even from your poverty, you can give me something. It may not seem like much, but it is the very thing I need. If you will give it to me I can do something I could not do without it.

"The sacrifices of God are a broken spirit: a broken and a contrite heart, O God, thou wilt not despise" (Ps. 51:17, KJV).

So, as best I could, I offered it up.

That was fifteen years ago. It has taken me a long time to assimilate this great lesson. I have not yet mastered it. But my understanding of sacrifice has been transformed. It has also transformed my life. The emphasis now is not on loss, privation, or a price to be paid. I see it as an act of intelligent worship, and as a gift God has given me to give back to Him *in order that He may make something of it.*

When Add died in September of 1973 the Lord in His mercy helped me to see a little more clearly in my second widowhood what I had only dimly descried in the first: a gift, a call, and a vocation, not merely a condition to be endured. Paul's words came alive: "Each one must order his life according to the gift the Lord has granted him" (1 Cor. 7:17, NEB).

So it was the Lord who had put into my hands this gift of

widowhood. Is this the little "cake" You need from me, Lord? Then I'll bake it for You, Lord. Please have it.

And what next? "I will offer ... the sacrifice of thanksgiving" (Ps. 116:17, NKJV). It is wonderfully comforting to be absolutely sure that we do the will of God. Here is one matter about which there can be no doubt: "Be thankful, whatever the circumstances may be. For this is the will of God for you in Christ Jesus" (1 Thess. 5:18, PHILLIPS).

Chapter Seventeen

The Glory of Sacrifice

As the widow of Zarephath busied herself to bake that little cake for Elijah, I wonder if she muttered something like, "What is he talking about? A handful of flour and a nearly empty cruse of oil—I'm supposed to make *two* cakes out of that? But—'Thus saith the Lord God of Israel.' Well, here's one stick. 'Thus saith the Lord God of Israel.' Over there's another one. Light the fire. Mix up the cake. We'll see."

When all we have to offer seems pitifully small and woefully poor, we must offer it nevertheless, in obedience like the widow's, and in the simplicity of a little child who brings a crushed dandelion to his mother. The child is not bitter and resentful at the poverty of his offering. He is happy to have *something*. Quantity and quality are not always under our control, and what the Lord can possibly make of it is no concern of ours. That part is under His control. He Himself knows what He will do. Let our offering be free, humble, unconditional, given in the full confidence that His transforming energy can fit it into the working of His purposes.

A few days after Addison Leitch proposed to me he wrote what I called his "geriatric letter." He was sixty, I was forty-two, and he did not want me entering into marriage to an old man with my eyes closed. He outlined some previews of coming attractions. The day would come, he predicted, when I would have to clean his glasses, take over the driving, and various other more onerous duties. Was I ready for that? His closing line was unforgettable:

"Yet here I am, all of me, for you, forever. *But what kind of an offer is that?*"

I accepted the offer. I loved him. Nothing else mattered. His predictions came true in exactly the order given, but love is a transformer.

When we give ourselves to God—"all of me, for You, forever"—or when we present to Him so apparently useless a thing as loneliness, what kind of an offer is that?

Never mind. Our offerings become a part of Christ's offering of Himself. He did it for love of the Father ("Lo, I come ... to do thy will, O God"; "Into thy hands I commend my spirit" [Heb. 10:7; Luke 23:46, KJV]). He did it also for love of us who so sorely needed it. Can we follow Him here, loving the Father enough to give ourselves wholly to Him, and putting ourselves out for love of those who do not seem (God forgive us for our pride!) to "deserve" it? "Live your lives in love—*the same sort of love* which Christ gives us and which he perfectly expressed when he gave himself up for us in sacrifice to God" (Eph. 5:2, PHILLIPS, italics added).

The same note is struck by the apostle Peter when he tells us that as we are built into a spiritual House of God, we become holy priests (we? holy priests? just imagine!) who may offer spiritual sacrifices, acceptable to God.[1] If the primary function of the priest is to offer sacrifice, then that is to be our primary function as His priests. The whole of life becomes a continual offering up for His praise.

Can we give up all for the love of God? When the surrender of ourselves seems too much to ask, it is first of all because our thoughts about God Himself are paltry. We have not really seen Him, we have hardly tested Him at all and learned how good He is. In our blindness we approach Him with suspicious reserve. We ask how much of our fun He intends to spoil, how much He will demand from us, how high is the price we must pay before He is placated. If we had the least notion of His loving-kindness and tender mercy, His fatherly care for His poor children, His generosity, His beautiful plans for us; if we knew how patiently He waits for our turning to Him, how gently He means to lead us to green pastures and still waters, how carefully He is preparing a place for us, how ceaselessly He is ordering and ordaining and engineering His Master Plan for our good—if we had any inkling of all this, could we be reluctant to let go of our smashed dandelions or whatever we clutch so fiercely in our sweaty little hands?

"We have not loved thee with our whole heart; we have not loved our neighbors as ourselves."[2]

If with courage and joy we pour ourselves out for Him and for others for His sake, it is not possible to lose, in any final sense, anything worth keeping. We will lose ourselves and our selfishness. We will gain everything worth having.

What if we hold back?

There is an old story of a king who went into the village streets to greet his subjects. A beggar sitting by the roadside eagerly held up his almsbowl, sure that the king would give handsomely. Instead the king asked the beggar to give him something. Taken aback, the beggar fished three grains of rice from his bowl and dropped them into the king's outstretched hand. When at the end of the day the beggar poured out what he had received, he found to his astonishment three grains of pure gold in the bottom of his bowl. *O that I had given him all!*

One aspect of sacrifice as seen in Scripture is glory. That element, though not always apparent, is always there. In the Old Testament we find the magnificent story of Abraham's obedience when asked to sacrifice his beloved son Isaac. What depths of suffering he endured for the love of God, what a revelation he was given of God's love for him, what a demonstration to every succeeding generation of the meaning of faith and obedience. There was none of this in his tortured mind as he climbed the mountain, no inkling of glory but only of a bloody holocaust. His father-heart endured agony because he loved his son and he loved his God.

But the glory followed—

Inasmuch as you have done this and have not withheld your son, your only son, I will bless you abundantly and greatly multiply your descendants until they are as numerous as the stars in the sky and the grains of sand on the sea-shore.... All nations on earth shall pray to be blessed as your descendants are blessed, and this because you have obeyed me.

GENESIS 22:16-18, NEB

When, long afterward under King Hezekiah, the house of the Lord was repaired and purified, there was a great celebration with sacrifices and music. At the moment when Hezekiah gave the order for the whole-offering to be laid on the altar and burnt, the singers began to sing, the trumpets sounded, the whole assembly prostrated themselves. Great joy accompanied great sacrifice. Why should it not be so for us also?

After the Crucifixion came the Resurrection. After the Resurrection the Ascension. Because Jesus wore a crown of thorns, He now wears a crown of glory. Because He became poor, He now sits enthroned. Because He made Himself of no reputation, He now has a name which is above every name. Because He was willing to become a slave, He is now Master of everything. Because He was obedient to death, He is Lord of Life and holds the keys of hell and of death. Because He made Himself of no reputation, every knee will someday bow before Him. Every renunciation led to glory.

God could not more fully and plainly show us the glorious truth of life out of death than in these paradoxes of Jesus' own life and death. Is it not clear to us that the sacrifice of Calvary was not a tragedy but the release of life and power? Do we believe this? How hard it is to believe that our own self-offering to Him will work in the same way. How easy it is for most of us to live as though we do not believe it.

He asks us to share with Him not only His Cross but also His glory. "If we died with him we shall also live with him: if we endure we shall also reign with him" (2 Tim. 2:12, PHILLIPS). And as Lilias Trotter's seed paintings show us, a deeper dying has endless powers of multiplying life in other souls.

Is He a hard Master to ask us to suffer with Him? Do we think it mean and unfair and unloving? But these are His *promises:*

"God ... fulfills his purpose for me."

"Thy wonderful purposes are all for our good."

"All things serve thee."

"Everything that happens fits into a pattern for good."

"In Christ ... we have been given our share in the heritage, as was decreed in his design whose purpose is everywhere at work. For it was his will that we, who were the first to set our hope on Christ, should cause his glory to be praised."

"Our mortal part may be absorbed into life immortal. God himself has shaped us for this very end."[3]

Six verses out of many which are divine guarantees. To take them into my heart as well as into my head alters my understanding of the meaning of life. If I am in Christ I really can't lose.

It is an old, old story. And it's mine, too. This is my story and this is my song. Jesus Christ has given me Living Water. Jesus Christ is my Bread. Jesus Christ is my Life. He is Jesu, Joy of Man's Desiring. I am the same body, the same temperament, with the same passions and the same history, but I know that all of those "givens" are capable of transformation. This is why

that old rugged Cross, so despised by the world,
holds a wondrous attraction for me.

Chapter Eighteen

A Share in Christ's Sufferings

Valerie called me last evening to ask for prayer for her ten-year-old son who had cried that morning because he feels very much alone at school, even though it is a Christian school. It was hard for him when the family left Mississippi to move to California, for he feared he would have no friends. He and I prayed together that God would give him a close friend in California. He has yet to find one, though nine months have gone by.

"Sometimes I think I should do the bad things the other kids do," he said, "just so they wouldn't think I was a goody-two-shoes. Maybe I should go ahead and talk dirty or disobey the teachers or something. I wish there was at least one guy on my side."

It wrung this grandmother-heart to think of the loneliness of that dear little boy. I asked the Lord to comfort him, and in some way to show him that this is a price he is paying for faithfulness, for which the Lord will one day reward him far beyond his dreams. I asked for wisdom for his parents, as they try to point him to the Cross.

Can God help this child to see beyond the schoolroom and the playground to things invisible? Can He show him this first hard lesson in what it means to take up the Cross? I believe He can. I pray that He will. The fact that His answer to the prayer for a friend has so far been No indicates to me that God does not think he needs the friend now—for God has promised to supply our needs. What we don't have now we don't need now. Possibly His very withholding is in order that the boy may learn, at this crucial juncture in his life, to turn to God in prayer for a deeply felt need.

When a man or woman, a boy or girl, accepts the way of loneliness for Christ's sake, there are cosmic ramifications. That person, in a secret transaction with God, actually does something for the life of the world. This seems almost inconceivable, yet it is true, for it is one part of the mystery of suffering which has been revealed to us.

The children who taunt Walter as "teacher's pet" because he does what is asked have no idea that God enters the picture at all. It is the last thing that would come to a child's mind without an older person's help. To submit to the authorities God puts over us is to submit to God. Rebellion is the spirit of what the Bible calls "the world," and we have the Lord's own Word for what Walter is suffering: "If you belonged to the world, the world would love its own; but because you do not belong to the world, because I have chosen you out of the world, for that reason the world hates you. Remember what I said: 'A servant is not greater than his master'" (John 15:19-20, NEB).

A hard obedience accepted for Christ is the Cross taken up. It is *His* Cross. He would not give us one which He Himself is not also bearing, has not also borne at Calvary. Each time my heart in love to Christ says YES when my human nature says NO, there the Cross is taken up. There I become a little more like my Master, there I live in Him, there I participate in His work of fulfilling the Father's will on earth.

For many years I thought of "suffering for Christ" as referring only to those forms of suffering which were the direct result of one's having witnessed publicly for Him or served Him in some specially significant way. I assumed that when Paul wrote to the Colossians, "It is now my happiness to suffer for you" (Col. 1:24, NEB), he referred to being in prison because of something he had done for their sakes. No doubt that was true, but not in the limited way I had thought. He meant far more. He saw the great truth of "exchange"—that out of his suffering would come good for others, meaning not only the church in Colosse. He goes on to say, "This is my way of helping to complete, in my poor human flesh, the full tale of Christ's afflictions still to be endured, for the sake of his body which is the church. I became its servant by virtue of the task assigned to me by God for your benefit" (Col. 1:24-25, NEB). While it is not difficult to see the task of an apostle as a divine assignment, it is often difficult to see our own as in any sense divinely assigned.

When Add died, one of his close friends, a minister whom I had never met, wrote to me that he believed I had been given "a vocation of suffering." The phrase seemed an overdramatization. I could think of thousands whose sufferings made mine look like nothing. But the forms of suffering we experience are not "electives." And while I could not *feel* that I had any special vocation, it was perhaps a *vocation* nevertheless. God had called me. He had called me to learn of Him by being alone—again. It was the thing appointed at the time.

If Paul could "fill up" or "complete," in his "poor human flesh, the full tale of Christ's afflictions," is it not possible that we also may do that? May not we too find real happiness in the quantum of our adversities, whether trivial or serious? Imagine being able to speak of suffering as happiness. We would dismiss it as nonsense or masochism if the apostle had not shown us that suffering is never useless but can, by grace, bless others. It has eternal ramifications when we are willing to receive it in faith. In every task assigned to us we become *helpers* in a great mystery which he calls the completion of a "tale." Our help affects the Body of Christ (the Church), and therefore, by extension, the whole world.

Although as the world looks at things, we may be "solo," we are not, as God looks at things, solitary instruments. We belong to an orchestra and make harmony by playing our particular part of the score on the instrument given us.

Or, to use the scriptural metaphor referred to above, Christians are like hands, feet, or eyes—parts of a body. Paul explains the operation of this mystical Body in simple terms of the human body—a harmony of many parts under one head, all contributing to the perfect working together of the whole. If one part should complain that because it is different from another, it doesn't belong in the body, that complaint will not change the facts. It does belong. If all parts had the same design and function, there would be no "body" at all. Unity is created out of diversity, not sameness. One part cannot accuse another of being superfluous simply because it isn't doing the same job.

> The eye cannot say to the hand, "I do not need you"; nor the head to the feet, "I do not need you." God has combined the various parts of the body, giving special honour to the humbler parts, so that there might be no sense of division in the body, but that all its organs might feel the same concern for one another.
>
> 1 CORINTHIANS 12:21, 24-25, NEB

Suppose the Supreme Designer sees that the Church, which *is* His Body, would not work properly, would not be harmonious and balanced, without single people. He sees that the Church *needs* them. And suppose their response is, "I don't want that role. I don't feel comfortable with that. Why should I be appointed as that particular piece of the mechanism? No thanks. My function in the Body must be my choice. So the 'humbler parts' have special honor? I'll forgo that distinction, thanks very much. The way things are now, I can't stand to be single. I can't take it."

What is that person saying? *My will be done.* I'll call myself a

Christian, but I don't accept the conditions. I'll serve, but only in the way I choose. I'll be the one calling the shots.

Even in these times when the emphasis is very much on careers for women, the "blueprint" still cherished by most of those who talk to me includes marrying Mr. Right, having a home and at least one or two children. The experience of one such woman was similar to my own:

Immature and terribly naive as to God's higher purposes, I could not see the loving "hedge" He had placed around me. Any male student for whom I had an infatuation never knew I existed. Any who liked me were not my type.

God's honing methods continue to vary but my struggles with singleness itself continue much as they ever have, with this one exception: I have made my peace with the future spectre of living all my days as a "spinster" or "old maid." Those two words and the connotations they evoked used to strike terror in my soul. At last, after years and years of running from the possibility that I may never know the love of a godly man, I told the Lord, "Yes. You'll just have to take care of me." Yet I must be honest and add that I still continue to hope celibacy will not always be my lot. Nevertheless I am quick to pray, "Not my will, Lord."

She goes on to describe "sick" feelings, feelings of rage, despair, panic, fainting. "I choke upon the awful taste of faithlessness. Dear God, help my unbelief." She tells of "mental skirmishes" when friends marry and bear healthy babies, recognizing in herself the resentment of the older brother of the Prodigal Son.

She revealed her soul to me on many more pages—a very human, womanly soul, striving hard to be honest. The fear of singleness was synonymous with the fear of a future in which she might not "feel fulfilled."

"Mrs. Elliot, are you able to perceive from these excerpts some of my internal conflicts and battles?" she asks.

Am I able? Dear God in Heaven, I am able! How completely I sympathize, for I've been there. It is for this very reason that I write to her about the whole mysterious and heavenly system of sacrifice which has so comforted me, has revealed to me the glory of sharing with Christ in His redemptive work. It has changed my response to life, with all its works, joys, and troubles. I am called close to the side of the Redeemer, given a small assignment which carries with it the power to *help complete* the quota or the tale of His own sufferings. The choice is mine.

Will you also go away? I hear Him say. *Or will you come with Me?*

Chapter Nineteen

A Strange Peace

Shortly before my daughter Valerie, my only child, went off to college as a freshman, that "sudden tide" came over me one morning as I was working in the kitchen. She had been the great joy of my life for seventeen years. When she was about eleven or twelve, friends heard me speak of what seemed to me a near-perfect mother-daughter relationship. "Oh, but wait till she's a teenager!" they warned. "Then you'll have some rough times." I was still waiting. I could not conceive of life without her.

"She has grown up," I told myself. "My job is finished, the job I loved more than anything else I have ever done. The nest is about to empty."

Overcome with sadness, I sat down at the wicker table, picked up the phone, and dialed Van, who is the sort of friend you don't have to explain things to. As I talked I began to cry.

"It's OK, Bet," she said quietly. "It'll be OK."

She did not need to explain to me what she meant. She knew

I understood. We believe the same things—things like *All shall be well, and all shall be well, and all manner of thing shall be well.*[1] But I needed to hear her say it. I needed to have the Word made flesh for me in her voice.

My soul was in turmoil that morning, presented with a new set of marching orders as Kathy's was when her youngest was going away. New circumstances would open new fields for trust, a new power to help "complete the tale," if only my response was YES.

Van's simple word, "It'll be OK," encouraged me to trust and obey. I learned that in this renunciation I had what the seed has that falls into the ground—a new potential for life-giving. I would be lonely, but I now had something precious to offer in love to my Lord, which in turn would make something quite different out of my loneliness. In some mysterious way which I could not predict, that offering would bring forth fruit. It would make a difference to the wholeness of the Body of which I was but a single member.

The "wholeness" of the Body. It dawned on me with new understanding—the wholeness of the Body is the holiness of the Body. A healthy body is healthy in all its parts. As each individual member grows in holiness, the Body grows in wholeness. Holiness is what matters to God. The holiness or the wholeness of one member of the Body makes a difference to all the rest.

The way I respond to the "givens" in my daily experience determines my growth in holiness. When we pray, "Give us this day our daily bread," God answers that prayer, measuring out just what we need for spiritual as well as physical growth. He knows that spiritual stamina cannot develop without conflict. We must take with both hands the thing given, submissively, humbly, sometimes courageously, or even, as one friend put it, "defiantly"—saying to ourselves, *This is part of the story*, the story of the love of God for me and of my love for Him.

This is acceptance in the truest sense. This is where real peace is found—that strange, inexplicable peace Jesus promised.

Rumer Godden, in her novel *In This House of Brede*, describes the meaning of a certain monastery's logo:

> The motto was *Pax*, but the word was set in a circle of thorns. Peace: but what a strange peace, made of unremitting toil and effort, seldom with a seen result; subject to constant interruptions, unexpected demands, short sleep at night, little comfort, sometimes scant food; beset with disappointments, and usually misunderstood; yet peace all the same, undeviating, filled with joy and gratitude and love. "It is My own peace I give unto you," not, notice, the world's peace.[2]

The only crown Jesus ever wore on earth was a crown of thorns.

What does that crown tell us about the love of God the Father? Much every way. For one thing, it tells us that His love is not a sentimental thing, for it was strong enough to hurt His own Son. He could have rescued Him with "legions of angels." He did not do so.

What does the crown of thorns tell us about the love of God the Son? It tells us that it was strong enough to deny itself, strong enough to suffer. He could have evaded the crown and the Cross. If He had taken Satan up on his offers in the wilderness He would have evaded both. He did not do so. He had set His face like a flint, and moved with flintlike resolution down that course, with all its humiliations, interruptions, demands, disappointments, and deprivations (this was the context of the peace He proffers us). He went straight to Jerusalem, and He went filled with joy and gratitude and love.

To be a Christian is to make the kind of choices which bring us daily into an ever greater and closer harmony with the Spirit of Christ. We cannot, indeed, be Christians at all unless we have within us that Spirit. As we make those choices in the freedom of the will God gave us, we find life and joy and peace. Jesus found His joy and peace, His very "meat," in the Father's will. The servant (may we never forget) is not "greater than his Master."

What if we choose to say NO?

It is a perilous choice. When Moses made his concluding charge to the people of Israel in Moab, he reviewed the history of God's faithfulness to them. Then he said,

> If there should be among you a man or woman, family or tribe, who is moved today to turn from the Lord our God and to go worshipping the gods of those nations—if there is among you such a root from which springs gall and wormwood, then when he hears the terms of this oath, he may inwardly flatter himself and think, "All will be well with me even if I follow the promptings of my stubborn heart"; but this will bring everything to ruin
>
> DEUTERONOMY 29:18-19, NEB.

This "root of bitterness" is mentioned also in Hebrews, following a passage which links holiness with peace. One who forfeits the grace of God is like a bitter, noxious weed which poisons the lives of others. Refusal to accept grace isolates, as a sulking child, wrapped up in his own misery, refuses comfort.

One evening when my grandson Jim Elliot Shepard was almost three, he found that his parents were going out and he was to be left with Granny. He began to cry, and when the door closed he threw himself on the floor in the hallway, kicking, screaming, beating his head on the carpet. I picked him up in my arms, which required no small effort as he stiffened and howled.

"Jim, would you like me to read you a story?"

Vigorous head shaking and howling.

"Let's go and rock in the big chair."

More howling.

"Jim, sweetheart—shall I get you some apple juice?"

The very personification of desolation and misery, he only roared and bellowed—"No! No! No! I want Mama!"

I tried everything and then, in my desperation, remembered to pray. Why hadn't I thought of that first? I asked the Lord to show me how to comfort him.

"Shall we go outside, Jim?"

Instantly he relaxed in my arms, turned his tear-stained face up to mine, and, choking with sobs, nodded Yes.

Still holding him in my arms, I opened the door to the carport. The heavy sweetness of jasmine filled the warm Mississippi night. He took a deep breath, as though inhaling the very peace of God. In a tiny whisper he said, "Granny—maybe we'll see some *stars.*"

I carried him into the backyard where we could look up through the trees. He was quiet for a long time, nestling into my shoulder, gazing silently at the spangled sky. Then— "Granny, those are *crickets* I hear. Do you hear them, Granny?"

The quest for satisfaction apart from the love of God is as futile as poor little Jim's refusal of the only comfort that was available to him that evening. He wanted Mama, and Mama was not there. Once he accepted what was offered, he came out of the howling wilderness of his misery and found peace.

My theme is oblation—the offering up of ourselves, all we are, have, do, and suffer. Sacrifice means something received and something offered.

But some may be wondering, *How,* exactly, do I do this? I hesitate to prescribe a method for so solemn and vital a spiritual transaction. God knows your heart and will accept your offering in any way you can make it, I am sure, but a very simple thing has helped me. It is to kneel with open hands before the Lord. Be silent for a few minutes, putting yourself consciously in His presence. Think of Him. Then think of what you have received in the four categories mentioned (are, have, do, suffer)— the gift of a child, for example, or, years later, the empty nest; the gift of work or the inability to work; marriage or singleness; pleasures or burdens; joy or sorrow. Next, visualize as well as you can this gift, resting there in your open hands. Thank the Lord for whatever aspect of this gift you can honestly thank Him for—if not for the thing in itself, then for its transformability, for His sovereignty, His will which allows you to have this gift, His unfailing love, the promise of His presence in deep waters and hot fires, the pattern for good which you know He is at work on. Then, quite simply, offer it up. Make God's gift to you your oblation to Him. Lift up your hands. This is a physical act denoting your love, your acceptance, your thanksgiving, and your trust that the Lord will make of it something redemptive for the wholeness of the Body, even for the life of the world.

Do not look for dramatic effects. There may be no discernible result. As my dear friend Frank Murray, an elder brother to me in the Lord, said regarding a matter we had prayed about, "It is a mistake to measure such things by introspection. He heard and answered. That is all there is to it. Let the answer be manifested in His own time and way."

I think you will begin to know the strange peace that is not the world's kind.

Chapter Twenty

Help Me Not to
Want So Much

Who of us has not known the pitched battle between the thirst for God and all that God wants for us—thirst like that of a hunted deer, gasping for the waterbrooks—and our very human, very earthy desires? As long as we live in this body of flesh and blood and passion, most of us will wrestle with these conflicting wants.

"My desire is to do thy will, O God, and thy law is in my heart" (Ps. 40:8, NEB) is our true prayer, yet we are simultaneously aware of many other desires. Once we have tasted the goodness of the Lord, our desire for Him is whetted. Once we have tasted the pleasures of the flesh, our desires for them are not easily abated.

A twice-divorced woman testified of her struggle to give God her physical hungers after "a lifetime of sexual activity." Tired of compromise which had never brought satisfaction, she wanted God's best, God's intimacy.

"My patterns are my enemy. The things the Lord impresses on me are 1. Put Him first; 2. Be still and know that He is God; 3. Progress, not perfection; 4. Continually give my thoughts and desires to Him; 5. Take time."

She was not sure why she was writing to me—"I guess just to air my doubts, seek encouragement and hope, but also to hear straight bottom-line how to start." I could add nothing to what the Lord had already shown her. Obedience to those five things would take her a long way. But the last line of her letter cried for an answer: "If only this would help me not to *want* so much! Will it? Eventually?"

The answer is yes—*eventually*. I can promise her that no one who trusts in God will be desolate. I can promise her that the more she drinks of the water Jesus gives (as opposed to all other kinds of thirst-quenchers), the more she will find it satisfies the *deepest* thirst. I can promise her that as she eats spiritual food she will acquire an ever-increasing taste for the Bread of Life, which fully satisfies the *deepest* hunger.

I can promise this because God promises it. I also know by experience that it is true. The operative word is *deepest*. Because our physical and emotional hungers are so strong, we easily imagine them to be our deepest hungers—until they are met, at which point we know that there is a bottomless one. It is that one God promises to meet. We must not demand from Him what He has not promised. Although He is a God of miracles, He does not promise miracles (by which I mean what C.S. Lewis means—an interference with nature by supernatural powers).

From graduation from college at twenty-one until I was twenty-six I waited for Jim Elliot, wishing that I wouldn't *want* him so much. I had no promises from him or from God that we would ever be married, but I was hungry for him—no, I was ravenous. Instead of taking away my appetite, the Lord showed me the indispensable lesson of Deuteronomy 8, a review of Israel's wilderness experience. While they craved for the food they had had in Egypt, God gave them manna. Manna was supernatural food, miraculously provided, and it was all they needed. But even a miracle did not stop the wanting of leeks, onions, garlic, watermelons, and fish. If He had given them what they naturally craved, they would never have learned to eat manna, they would never have acquired a taste for the bread which came down from heaven. God *made them hungry* on purpose—in order to humble and test them, to discover whether it was in their hearts to obey Him, and to teach them what was far more important than leeks and onions: that man does not live by those things alone, but by the Word of the Lord. "The Lord your God was disciplining you as a father disciplines his son."[1]

So He disciplines us. He pays us that "intolerable compliment" of loving us inexorably. He harrows our souls, making us long for something we cannot have, in order to reveal to us what He wants us to have, which in the long run is far better.

"If only this would help me not to *want* so much!" My correspondent knows she must continually give God her thoughts and desires. But immediate effects are not always visible. She may keep on wanting for a long time.

One day when Jesus was on His way to Jerusalem, somebody asked Him if only a few people would be saved. His answer did not deal with the percentage, which was none of their business any more than it is ours. He made clear what *is* our business: "You must try your hardest to get in through the narrow door, for many, I assure you, will try to do so and will not succeed" (Luke 13:24, PHILLIPS).

From another recent letter:

I am confronted with that same troublesome mystery—suffering, pain, and tears are a part of God's economy on earth. The truth just *sickens* me! There is no growth and no fruit apart from pain. Christianity is not for the weak, although the world would have us believe so. It is for those who find the courage to humble themselves.

It is a small door we must get through. I wanted to encourage both of these women to see that the small door opens up to a very large place. If they believe that, they will certainly find the courage to humble themselves. I have not heard again from the first, but the second has prayed, "Be it unto me according to Thy word."

Sometimes we prefer to "struggle" even when we are quite clear about what we ought to do. Struggling in such a case only postpones obedience. While we play for time, we can put off the moment of terrible choice. Sooner or later someone is bound to come along and say just what we hoped to hear, "Go with your feelings." That may seem the easiest way until we try it, whereupon we find that feelings are always cancelling each other out—which ones shall we go with? When we have once met God we know there's a war on. We have a lower nature that sets its desires against the Spirit.

"Anyone can see the kind of behaviour that belongs to the lower nature: fornication, impurity, and indecency; idolatry and sorcery; quarrels, a contentious temper, envy, fits of rage, selfish ambitions, dissensions, party intrigues, and jealousies" (Gal. 5:19-21, NEB). Those who go with feelings like that will never inherit the kingdom of God.

You would not have read so far in this book if you were one who in your heart of hearts wants to go with feelings like that. You want what Paul calls "the harvest of the Spirit"—love, joy, peace, patience, kindness, goodness, fidelity, gentleness, self-control. You can't have it both ways.

Great literature, which holds up a mirror in which, with a shock of recognition, we see ourselves, portrays the deep conflicts that result from good desires contending with evil ones. The great characters of the Bible had great struggles. It is the Spirit in us, Paul explains, that fights against the lower nature. Sometimes, alas, we imagine that the Spirit is fighting against *us* and our deepest longings. We picture God as a spoilsport, when in fact His Spirit contends against the sin in us which will prevent our ever having what will bring us the greatest happiness.

The story of a girl I'll call Millie illustrates how easily we cheat and deceive ourselves when we do what we "feel like" doing. She had been a Christian for nearly fifteen years, and thought of herself as "basically old-fashioned." But, like most other young people, she had a tough time trying to stay pure.

She met a very attractive non-Christian, went out with him "too many times," allowed him the liberties he felt he had a right to, and soon found things out of control. "I feel so STU-PID!" she told me, "I could just kick myself!" Rationalizing all along, the pair indulged in various kinds of sexual play. Millie told herself that as long as there was no actual sexual intercourse she could still call herself a virgin.

"So I did everything else" (and here she went into lurid detail). "I am so *ashamed*."

Far from bringing her the love and happiness she had longed for, this course of action made Millie utterly miserable. Although a year had passed since the man disappeared, she still fought overwhelming guilt and self-hatred. She knew the Scriptures—that Jesus died for her, that His blood could wash away all her sin, "nothing is too awful for Him to forgive." She had confessed it all to Him. She was sorry—couldn't be sorrier. Yet she was tormented by the thought that she could never be worthy of the kind of Christian man she had always dreamed of marrying. Was she lying to herself to think she was still a virgin? *Filthy* was the only word to describe how she felt.

She had read my book *Passion and Purity* twice. "You are so *right on the money!*" she said, "That's why I thought you might help me."

My heart went out to her. Her loneliness had opened the gates of her soul, as it were, and let in the wild beasts of sexual sin. She was drawn by temptations she might otherwise have been immune to, and because she had yielded, was filled with guilt, shame, and fear. So many have written of similar experiences and the same deep regrets—sickened, wanting to kick themselves, ashamed, couldn't be sorrier. I have tried to assure them of the total forgiveness promised to those who truly repent. No sin is great enough to drain dry the ocean of God's grace.

Having said that, we must also say that sins have consequences which God Himself does not necessarily undo. Virginity is a gift even God cannot give back. He gave it once, to be given once—in marriage. If marriage is not in His will, virginity is His will. When it has been squandered it is not restored. It is possible to squander sexual purity in many ways besides "technical" intercourse. This is why it is of such huge importance to draw the line very far on this side. The only really safe rule is *hands off, clothes on.* One thing leads rapidly to another, until one can no longer offer oneself whole and unspoiled to a prospective wife or husband. When one of the opposite sex has been "known," he or she cannot be "unknown." A choice has been made. It cannot be unmade.

That's the bad news. Here's the good news. It's about Amazing Grace. Though the Lord cannot restore virginity, He will restore purity to the heart that has confessed and forsaken the sin. The blood of Jesus Christ *cleanses.* It cleanses from *all* sin.

The Church at Corinth was like every other church in Christian history—a motley collection of sinners. Churches, because they are made up of human beings, are full of human beings' problems. Paul wrote two long letters to the Corinthians to help sort them out. He said this:

Make no mistake: no fornicator or idolater, none who are guilty either of adultery or of homosexual perversion, no thieves or grabbers or drunkards or slanderers or swindlers, will possess the kingdom of God. Such were some of you. But you have been through the purifying waters; you have been dedicated to God and justified through the name of the Lord Jesus and the Spirit of our God.... Your body is a shrine of the indwelling Holy Spirit.... You do not belong to yourselves; you were bought at a price.

1 CORINTHIANS 6:9-11, 19, 20, NEB

To those who ask for help in receiving the complete pardon Christ offers, I usually say something like this: Make a habit of consciously putting your mind on what Christ has done for you, not on what *you've* done. Praise Him, memorize Scripture and hymns, pray, and follow Him in obedience. Even if the memory of the sins comes back, don't worry about it. Bring those thoughts "into captivity to the obedience of Christ" (2 Cor. 10:5, NKJV).

"But holy cow!" a young man said to me after he'd read *Passion and Purity*. "You gotta have sex!" Who says so? Thousands of Christians and others have lived out their lives without any sexual experience whatsoever. Chastity not only does no harm to one's person, but strengthens one's manhood or womanhood. It does not diminish and despoil, but actually ennobles character. The greater the restraint, the greater the power. Self-mastery, as someone has said, is the *greatest virility*.

Self-control is included in the list of fruits of the Spirit. *Self-*

control. The Holy Spirit does not do all the controlling for us. He requires us to act. He helps us, but He expects us to co-operate. I believe that if we begin by the complete offering of ourselves in the particular willed action of oblation described in foregoing chapters, we thereby put ourselves under His authority and power. If we begin each day by an acknowledgment of our dependence upon Him, and our intention to obey Him, He will certainly help us. The Holy Spirit, who is the source of our life, then directs the course. Every discipline imposed in that course is for one purpose: "to bring us to our full glory," and to make us "part of the permanent" that "cannot die" (1 Cor. 2:8, NEB; 1 John 2:17, PHILLIPS).

Chapter Twenty-One

Turn Your Solitude
Into Prayer

Only one sentence from all that was said at a certain retreat remains in my mind. That one sentence was worth the weekend: Turn your loneliness into solitude, and your solitude into prayer.

We have noted that aloneness was not a painful thing until sin entered the world. Loneliness now means pain. The other aspect of aloneness, solitude, need not mean pain. It may mean glory.

Loneliness is a wilderness, but through receiving it as a gift, accepting it from the hand of God, and offering it back to Him with thanksgiving, it may become a pathway to holiness, to glory, and to God Himself.

We hear people speak of wanting freedom—from the familiar, from responsibility, from everything—in order to "find" themselves. I wonder how many could clearly explain what they mean by that finding, or what they would do if the quest were successful. When one has found "himself" what has he found? What does he do next? The revelation of the self is a horrifying thing unless there is another to turn to. Albert Camus described it in *The Fall:*

> Alone in a forbidding room, alone in the prisoner's box before the judges, and alone to decide in face of oneself or in the face of others' judgment. At the end of all freedom is a court sentence; that's why freedom is too heavy to bear, especially when you're down with a fever, or are distressed, or love nobody.
>
> Ah, *mon cher,* for anyone who is alone, without God and without a master, the weight of days is dreadful. Hence, one must choose a master, God being out of style.[1]

The prophet Isaiah experienced what it is to be alone before God. It happened, he tells us, in the year that King Uzziah died. There was a connection in his mind, surely, between the two events.

Uzziah had reigned for fifty-two years, during many of which he did what was right in the eyes of the Lord as Amaziah his father had done. He set himself to seek God's guidance. He took instruction from Zechariah in the fear of God, and as long as he pursued this course God made him prosper. He gained tremendous power in the military field, having an army of 307,500 men, equipped with shields, spears, helmets, coats of mail, bows, and sling-stones. He had his engineers design machines for discharging arrows and rocks. He became very famous, then he became very proud, presuming to enter the temple and usurp the place of the priests in burning incense. God struck him down with disease so that he had to live out the rest of his days not in royal splendor but as a leper. Even his burial was ignominious—not with the kings but in a burial-ground.

Isaiah must have thought long and hard about this man's life—his fame, his power, his reign, his pride, his exile in leprosy, his lonely death. What had he to show for it all? Possibly Isaiah had Uzziah in mind when he wrote, "Mankind is brought low, men are humbled, humbled are haughty looks. But the Lord of Hosts sits high in judgement, and by righteousness the holy God shows himself holy" (Isa. 5:15-16, NIV). No doubt the prophet sensed the great loneliness we all feel when we contemplate death—the most solitary of solitary things. No one can share it. A man dies alone. Alone he goes out into the unknown.

Sometime during that year of the king's death Isaiah found solitude. He did not record where or how, but he told us what he saw: *the Lord,* seated on a throne, high and exalted, attended by seraphim ceaselessly calling, "Holy, holy, holy, is the Lord of Hosts: the whole earth is full of his glory" (Isa. 6:5, NEB). As their voices thundered and reverberated with the solemn words, the threshold shook to its foundations, and the house was filled with smoke. This vision of holiness shook not only the house but also the prophet himself to the very foundations. He had had ample opportunity to witness the wrongs of Uzziah's life and, if he was so inclined, to make comparisons with his own. But when he saw the holiness of God, comparisons between himself and other men fell away. He cried out that he was a lost man, a man who, because with his own eyes he had seen the King, saw at the same time the truth about himself. He was a sinner. Fortunately for him God was not "out of style," as He was for Camus' protagonist. Fortunately he knew his Master.

In solitude Isaiah saw the Lord. In solitude he found himself and the revelation was more than he could bear. "What a wretched state I am in! I am lost!"

So it is with all who enter into real solitude. The layers of acquired knowledge, conditioned behavior, and self-confidence are sloughed off. The vision of the self without all its accustomed accretions is shocking. How different from the cherished image does the authentic self appear!

> "When I'm alone"—the words
>   tripped off his tongue
> As though to be alone were
>   nothing strange.
> "When I was young," he said,
>   "when I was young ..."
> I thought of age, and loneliness
>   and change,
> I thought how strange we grow
>   when we're alone,
> And how unlike the selves that
>   meet and talk,
> And blow the candles out, and
>   say goodnight.

Alone ... The word is life
   endured and known.
It is the stillness where our
   spirits walk
And all but inmost faith is
   overthrown.

Siegfried Sassoon[2]

I do not know Sassoon's inmost faith, but I know Isaiah's. Faced with the truth of the unknown self, so disquieting in its strangeness, Isaiah knew where to turn. Standing in the Uncreated Light he knew himself to be naked, guilty, and powerless. There was nothing for him to do but to cast himself on God's mercy. And mercy met him, not with sympathy but with cleansing fire.

It takes the fire of God to cleanse our hearts of selfishness in all its subtle forms. Even loneliness may be a form of selfishness. One can reject friendship when it is not offered on the terms one chooses. One can reject the grace of God as Naaman the leper came perilously close to doing because it was not offered with the kind of ceremony he felt befitted his station. One can magnify his loneliness out of all proportion, as though he suffered something that is not common to man, forgetting that "this is life"—not more, not less. One can draw about himself a thick quilt of self-pity and isolate himself in other ways, but if one turns the loneliness into solitude and the solitude into prayer, there is release. It may require a willingness to be burned if burning is necessary as it was for Isaiah, but there is forgiveness and cleansing and peace. In Isaiah's case, this was followed by God's call for a volunteer to work for Him. With a heart at leisure now from itself, Isaiah could answer, "Here I am. Send me."

I was pondering this matter when the Lord brought straight to my kitchen table yesterday a living example of such a heart. A bright young woman and I were eating lamb sandwiches. I asked her if she is lonely.

"Lonely? Why should I be?"

"You're single. Most of the single people I know talk about being lonely."

With a look of surprise and then a laugh she said, "Oh no. You see, I have a sense of expectancy every day. What does the Lord want to do with me today? I have no agenda of my own."

No agenda of my own. There is the key to Linda's freedom. I continued to question her. Yes, she said, she knows what loneliness feels like—it's isolation, when you think you can't reach anybody, nobody reaches you, you're cut off. You have your own agenda.

"What do you mean by an agenda?" I asked.

"Thinking there's only one solution and God has to give you that or nothing. You have a closed mind. A closed mind is a closed heart and a closed door."

Now I recognized the reason for the smile which seems always to light Linda's face. I think it must come from her wholehearted acceptance of *God's* "agenda."

"I love solitude," she said. "As I drove up here this morning [it was a dazzling winter morning of sunshine and blue sky and blue shadows on the snow] I didn't have the radio on. I wasn't listening to tapes. I was just quiet. I love times like that."

The heart which has no agenda but God's is the heart at leisure from itself. Its emptiness is filled with the Love of God. Its solitude can be turned into prayer.

Chapter Twenty-Two

How Do I Do This
Waiting Stuff?

One discipline of the spiritual life to which many of us find it most difficult to submit is that of waiting. No other discipline reveals more about the quality of our faith than that one. Sometimes we are subject to criticism from others because we seem to be doing nothing. When waiting is an act of obedience it is of course an invisible one. Only the One waited on sees it for what it is, but we must resist the temptation to defend and explain to our critics, and simply go on trusting.

True waiting on God is not "doing nothing." Psalm 37 lists the principal elements of this hidden activity, a perfect formula for peace of mind (parentheses not divinely inspired, merely mine):

Trust in the Lord and do good.

Dwell in the land (make your home, settle down, be at peace where God puts you).

Delight in the Lord (make the Lord your only joy) and He will give you what your heart desires.

Commit your life to the Lord.

Trust in Him and He will act.

Be quiet before the Lord.

Wait patiently for Him, not worrying about others.[1]

Waiting patiently is almost impossible unless we also are learning at the same time to find joy in the Lord, commit everything to Him, trust Him, and be quiet. My friend Liz recognizes her need to learn the steps. She writes:

I would love to ask you the "how to's" of this whole daily exercise of faith. Being single. But I hope that my hoping and wrestling in this "love arena" will be won out WITH HIM on the curve of daily life. The rigors of the battle of learning these steps of faith will suffice more than a catalogue of answers.

It seems much too easy for me to sit down and write out some casual note that screams "How do I do this waiting stuff?" when God has set up an order of commands, laws, guidelines that mark my path quite clearly.... PRAYER is the greatest "reasoning" I could request.

I pray for her and for the multitudes like her who struggle to wait. I think of the story told by Amy Carmichael in her first year of missionary work in Japan. She and a missionary couple were held up on a journey because of a boat which did not arrive or did not leave—I forget which. Not just hours but days went by, and the young missionary began to fret because of the time lost and the consequences to others who counted on them. The older missionary said calmly, "God knows all about the boats." It became a maxim of faith for the rest of her life.

Many times in my life God has asked me to wait when I wanted to move forward. He has kept me in the dark when I asked for light. To my pleas for guidance His answer has often been *Sit still, My daughter.* I like to see progress. I look for evidence that God is at least doing something. If the Shepherd leads us beside still waters when we were hoping for "white water" excitement, it is hard to believe anything really vital is taking place. God is silent. The house is silent. The phone doesn't ring. The mailbox is empty. The stillness is hard to bear—and God knows that. He knows our frame and remembers we are made of dust. He is very patient with us when we are trying to be patient with Him. Of course for most of us this test of waiting does not take place in a silent and empty house, but in the course of regular work and appointments and taxpaying and grocery buying and trying to have the car fixed and the storm windows up; daily decisions have to go on being made, responsibilities fulfilled, families provided for, employers satisfied. How can we speak of waiting on God in the middle of all that? How be still?

There is a secret place where the Christian dwells. It is the shadow of the Almighty. Transactions take place there which none but God know.

A tiny scrap of lined notebook paper says this:

I just want to thank you for preaching simply the *Cross.*
Please never stop proclaiming it. I must die daily to have resurrection life in my calling.... So you might want to pray for
me, if you think of it. I'm a very young girl with a very big
test of faith and obedience before me. I know I am in His will
now in this area, and the Lord has ministered to me so specially, but obedience doesn't always tickle.

These are letters from women. It seems to me there is one
aspect of waiting on God in the matter of marriage that is different for women than for men. I cannot prove my conclusions,
but I offer the reasons for those conclusions for your consider-
ation.

The archetypal feminine characteristic is receptivity, as we can
learn from the human form (the female body is made to
receive), and from the Genesis account of creation (the woman
was made for the man). Because all human creatures are
dependent on God for life, the soul (whether that of a man or
a woman) is a receptor, and therefore has always been viewed as
feminine. God is always the initiator in the soul's relation to
Him. We are receivers of God's grace and responders to Him in
gratitude. The metaphor of Bridegroom and Bride is used in
Scripture to describe the relationship between God and His
people—God the Creator, the great Initiator, His people the
receivers of all. "God is so masculine," said C.S. Lewis, "that all
creation is feminine by comparison."

As those who represent the Bride in the great Mystery of
Marriage, women have a special reason to wait on God. They

were not created for *headship* in the special way that men were. Therefore it seems reasonable that if God wants a woman to marry, He will see to it that the man finds her. She need not go out hunting (I didn't, and three of them found me). When I was a little girl my parents told me that if I got lost in a crowd, I was to stand still in one place and they would find me. If both they and I were searching, we might miss each other. So might a man and a woman.

St. Teresa of Jesus distills the very essence of submissive waiting in these words:

Let nothing trouble thee.

Let nothing frighten thee.

All things pass away.

God never changes.

Patience obtains all things.

Nothing is wanting to him who possesses God.

God alone suffices.

The man, I think, has a different responsibility when it comes to marriage. He ought to do the searching. This may be a quirky prejudice of my own just because it was what my mother always told me and it certainly worked in my case, but then again it might have something to do with The Way Things Are, an arrangement that goes back to the beginning of time.

Adam did not go out looking for a woman. There weren't any. He didn't know what a woman was. When God decided it was not a good thing for him to be alone, He then made all the wild animals and all the birds of heaven. Adam named them all, and the account gives me the impression that he and God were surveying each animal or bird to see whether it might make a companion for him, "but for the man himself no partner had yet been found." So God custom-made that needed partner, brought her to Adam to "husband"—to be her protector and provider.

Most marriages, in most of human history, I suppose, have been arranged. Abraham sent a servant to find a wife for his son Isaac. It is still the custom in many parts of the world, India, Africa, and China among them, but the modern American can hardly conceive of such a thing, in spite of the far higher rate of success of that method than of our do-it-yourself.

Am I recommending a return to the ancient way? I would like to, but I refrain. Instead I would say that if a man is to walk with God, surely he needs to come to grips, *before* he enters into any emotional involvements with women, with whether or not marriage is a part of his God-given task. If it is, then the pattern shows that he is to love his wife as Christ loved the Church. He must begin as Christ does, by wooing and winning, by calling her to himself, risking rejection, taking the initiative, sacrificing himself. It's a serious business. Before tackling it he should submit himself to the disciplines of Psalm 37 as given above. When these are skipped, confusion and heartbreak result.

Two months after Jim Elliot and I had talked about the gift of singleness he sat one rainy November morning at his desk, gazing glumly out at the soaked side yard of his parents' house. It was during his year of "waiting." He was desperate to get to his mission work in South America, but felt he needed to wait for a year in order to study, to be at home and be quiet, and to

be under the spiritual tutelage of his father, as Timothy was
under the apostle Paul. To make matters more difficult, he was,
to use the current phrase, "emotionally involved." He called it
being in love. He wondered sometimes if he had run ahead of
God in letting me know it. It had certainly complicated his life
and mine. Yet he was still praying and waiting for guidance, trying to be obedient and finding that it didn't "tickle." Long after
God had given him the answer I found these lines in his hand-
writing, with the date, November 10, 1949:

May I then not know her love
Up close, her warm, unhindered flesh
Against my own? Must rather feel
Wind-kisses, and watch
The twining of the vines on forest trees?
Must see in these the emblems of it all?
Oh, must I still walk woodsy paths alone,
And push quietly to rest
With cast-off pine needles?

Caress, wind;
Sigh, you firs;
Cling closely, vines;
Warm one another, naked needles:
Die, love within.

Oh, fiery anguish of the passion-flame
Of youth, I beg of you,

Be quelled. Cease
Spitting embers through my frame.
And you, daughters of Jerusalem,
Wherever you may be,
Run to your Lord and tell Him,
Tell Him now for me
That I am sick of love.

Obviously Jim had been saturating himself in the great love-poem of the Bible, the Song of Solomon. He had been encouraged by a chapel speaker in college not to stir up or awake love "until it please," which the speaker took to refer to God's timing, which is always perfect. While Jim waited for that time, he determined to discipline his behavior toward me and the expression of his desire, but he did not refuse to acknowledge plainly before *God* the workings of his heart. This can be a source of great comfort, far more comfort than the neurotic effort to insulate oneself from reality, refusing to be touched by it. Take it honestly to Him who is "no High Priest who cannot sympathize with our weaknesses—he himself has shared fully in all our experience of temptation, except that he never sinned" (Heb. 4:15, PHILLIPS). He will understand.

The kind of waiting I refer to here is not mere marking time because of timidity, or "the indecision that can make no choice, the irresolution that carries no choice into act."[2] Waiting on God is an act of faith—the greatest thing ever required of us humans. Not faith in the outcome we are dictating to God, but faith in His character, faith in Himself. It is resting in the perfect confidence that He will guide in the right way, at the right time. He will supply our need. He will fulfill His word. He will give us the very best if we trust Him.

A woman's waiting, regarding the question of marriage, means leaving the whole thing in God's hands. A man's waiting means asking whether he should plan for marriage. He may need to wait a long time for a yes or no. I would suggest that he give up dating until he knows. It will be much easier to concentrate.

If the answer seems to be yes, it is a good idea to ask older Christians who can keep their mouths shut to pray for you. Ask them for specific suggestions as to someone they think suitable. Take their suggestions seriously. Move in the direction of the will of God.

I met Lars, the man who was to become my husband, the day after my second husband, Add, died. He had just arrived as a student at Gordon-Conwell Theological Seminary where Add had been a professor. He went to a chapel service in which various people spoke of what Add had meant to them. I said a few words, and Lars took note.

Years later a casual friendship had developed into (in *his* mind) something more. He came often to see me, occasionally took me to dinner, brought me flowers. Any woman understands these gestures, but we never spoke of a "relationship." It took me a long time to consider him as anything but a very easy-to-have-around friend. I could not imagine a third marriage. But when I saw that he was moving toward a proposal, I had to get down to business and pray about what my answer should be. I was middle-aged, of course, and had been through this twice before, but there are no "experts" in prayer and faith. It was the same slow and certain light I had to seek and wait for. I not only prayed and waited, but also asked counsel of several godly people who knew both of us.

My prayers brought an unlooked-for answer. I began to detect in my heart a wholly new sort of interest in this man. In addition to the gentlemanliness and charm which had been obvious in our first meeting, I saw a servant-heart. I saw his own great tact and care in his treatment of me as a woman and a widow. Like Jim and Add, he was manly. Manliness has always touched a very deep chord in me. I was impressed, too, with his willingness to wait, so quietly and so long. More than four years after that chapel service where he saw me he asked me to marry him.

Waiting is an offering and a sacrifice. We may lift up our very waiting to Him as a daily oblation, in a spirit of expectancy— like Linda's, who asks daily only for God's agenda. Waiting on God in *this* way is true faith—no agenda of one's own, no deadlines, no demands on what God must do. Simply an open heart and open hands ready to receive that which God shall choose, and a perfect confidence that what He chooses will be better than our best. God takes the part of that kind of soul.

"Never has ear heard or eye seen any other god taking the part of those who wait for him. Thou dost welcome him who rejoices to do what is right" (Isa. 64:4-5, NEB).

Chapter Twenty-Three

A Pathway to Holiness

The wildernesses spoken of in the Bible were usually very barren places, but God can change that. He can make streams in the desert, springs in the valley, and furnish tables in the wilderness. The wilderness of loneliness is a place where charity may blossom. "Fill up the emptiness of your heart with love for God and your neighbor," wrote Edith Stein, whose love made even a concentration camp a place of joy.

Those whose lives have had the deepest spiritual impact in the world are those who have suffered. In God's mysterious providence, the Cross and the crown, suffering and glory, are linked. History is replete with stories of martyrdom, beginning with Stephen who, as the rocks rained on him from the angry crowd, fell on his knees and prayed for the rock-throwers. God did not save him from death, but his death impressed a fanatical bystander who later turned into an apostle. Beethoven, deprived of the one faculty which would seem indispensable to a musician, his hearing, went on to write even greater symphonies.

This book will not be read by great martyrs or composers, yet their stories should put heart into us. Our own diminishments, in God's sovereign ordering of all things for His glory and our good, are not only the prerequisites to our own joy, but may also be the means of enriching the lives of others.

A story of such diminishment and enrichment comes to me from a girl in her twenties. It begins in the usual way—she met "a very special young man." Both were dedicated to God, longing to know and serve and please Him. They worked at the same job, went to the same church, and when they were attracted to each other, agreed on strict physical restraint. The attraction increased, they spoke of the possibility of marriage, Christian counselors encouraged them to marry, but he could not come to a decision. After what seemed to the girl more than a reasonable length of time for a man to make up his mind, they parted. He was lost to her, "probably forever."

Combined with this "loss" is the string of disappointments, the emptiness of aloneness, his absence, and the temptation to cry WHY? I have tried to live life without skipping a beat and trust God with the questions and pain, leaving my burdens at the Cross.

And what has happened? Not the miracle of an instant change of feelings, but the miracle of life out of death—the transformation of one woman's diminishment into the enrichment of others. In working with the youth group in her church, even on days when she felt she had nothing whatever to give them because of her own wounds,

The things I've heard come out of my mouth in the last few weeks I know were sent from above! He promises to heal the brokenhearted, and I cling to those promises now!!

Love, it seems, *creates* good—by drawing good out of any situation through suffering. The suffering itself thereby becomes a pathway to holiness. St. Paul writes to his beloved Corinthians:

The all-merciful Father, the God whose consolation never fails us ... comforts us in all our troubles, so that we in turn may be able to comfort others in any trouble of theirs and to share with them the consolation we ourselves receive from God. As Christ's cup of suffering overflows, and we suffer with him, so also through Christ our consolation overflows. If distress be our lot, it is the price we pay for your consolation, for your salvation; if our lot be consolation, it is to help us to bring you comfort, and strength to face with fortitude the same sufferings we now endure.

2 CORINTHIANS 1:3-6, NEB

Out of suffering comes holiness—in these forms: comfort, consolation, the fellowship of Christ's suffering, salvation, strength, fortitude, endurance. This is what is meant by redemptive suffering. The greater the measure allotted to us, the greater is our material for sacrifice. As we make it a joyful offering to God, our potential is enhanced for becoming "instruments of His Peace"—being "broken bread and poured-out wine," overflowing with consolation for the lonely and the suffering of the world.

Do we want to be servants to one another in love? Let God turn even our loneliness into power to serve. Let Him free us from ourselves in order that we may become the servants of others. As the basis of our union with Christ is His sacrificial love for us, so the basis of our union with others is that same sort of love—the love that forgets itself and its own troubles and lays itself down.

It would be preposterous for me to pretend that I know very much about this by practice. I do not. In the first place, in the scale of human sufferings my own do not appear to me to have been great. In the second place, every fresh vision of the Love of God and every reading of the Love Chapter, 1 Corinthians 13, show me how far I am from the daily practice of that kind of love.

So although I write of things of which I know only a little by experience, even a very little draws back the curtain enough to reveal to me that God meant just what He said. He promises

> garlands instead of ashes, oil of gladness instead of mourners' tears, a garment of splendour for a heavy heart.... And so, because shame in double measure and jeers and insults have been my people's lot, they shall receive in their own land a double measure of wealth, and everlasting joy shall be theirs.
>
> ISAIAH 61:3, 7, NEB

The Scriptures abound with these exchanges, for instance: pine trees instead of camel thorn, myrtles for briars, blessings for curses, dancing for laments, joy for sackcloth, pastures for wilderness, light for darkness, God's guidance for our confusion, the filling of our own needs when we fill others', the kingdom of heaven in place of poverty, comfort for mourning, satisfaction for hunger and thirst, rewards in heaven for persecutions on earth, an imperishable body in place of a perishable one, power in place of weakness, glory for humiliation, immortality for mortality, a resplendent body for a vile one, and—the culmination of all—life out of death.

In the seventeenth century George Herbert wrote this dialogue between Christian and Death:

Christian
Alas, poore Death! where is thy glorie?
Where is thy famous force, thy ancient sting?

Death
Alas, poore mortall, void of storie!
Go spell and reade how I have killed thy King.

Christian
Poore Death! and who was hurt thereby?
Thy curse being laid on Him makes thee accurst.

Death
Let losers talk, yet thou shalt die;
These arms shall crush thee.

Christian
Spare not, do thy worst:
I shall be one day better than before;
Thou so much worse, that thou shalt be no more.[1]

"Better than before." The Lord has come to wipe away tears, the Bible tells us, and we may take that to mean He has come to dispel loneliness. He will dispel it—as soon as He can, not before. The tears, the loneliness, the pains of this life are a part of the process He is at work on. If we understand that, we need never be bitter about it. It will one day be exchanged for wholeness. This is why we can sing, even about death, as Herbert did: *Spare not, do thy worst.*

Chapter Twenty-Four

Spiritual Maturity Means Spiritual Parenthood

It may seem to some readers that this treatment of human loneliness is only theoretical, perhaps merely passive, perhaps "too spiritual." Where is the *practical* help?

I might suggest that you join a health club or the church choir or go on a cruise; take an evening class in poetry or underwater basketweaving; learn to sing, ski, sew, snorkel, or spelunk. If you're looking for a husband, move to Alaska—that's where the men are, they say. If it's a wife you want, go to the foreign mission field. Single women greatly outnumber the men there (in Ecuador when I was there it was something like seventy to one).

But of course I am suggesting nothing along that line. It is a very different line that I offer, more practical, more "useful" in the long run than any diversion, one that has been for me not only eminently workable wherever I was, whatever the cause, but fundamentally transforming. It is not a trick or a program or a method of getting rid of loneliness altogether. I do not believe there is such a thing. It does not cost money, require skill, or depend upon the cooperation of others. It is this simple matter of seeing loneliness as a gift—to be received, and to be offered back to God for His use. We might say it is *coin*, exchangeable for something of everlasting value.

When a coin is spent it's gone. I have often found that loneliness given to God disappears. I cannot find it anywhere. My heart is light. My work is a joy. I am healed. And all unbeknownst to me, there has been, in addition to my own healing, an exchange I did not dream of: Someone else's load has been lightened.

But then it comes again, in a different way, perhaps, but loneliness all the same—the reminder that I was made for God, my heart will never rest anywhere else, and nothing the world can offer will satisfy.

Can I promise that your loneliness will disappear at once? No. It does not always happen so. I cannot offer a wand which when waved in the proper way will make your troubles vanish. I cannot say, "This is what you can do about it," but I can say, "This is what you can do *with* it—right now." Receive it willingly as from God. Offer it thankfully back to God.

You will still be alone, but you will not be lonely. You will find solace in solitude, and your oblation brings you one step nearer to spiritual maturity.

* * *

But I want to go a step further. It is more than a step, I think. It is a door which is open to all of us—that of spiritual parenthood.

Physical maturity brings the power to reproduce. Spiritual maturity brings the same. I believe we are meant to be fathers and mothers. Not all of us in the usual physical way, for God's original plan was botched. When we are redeemed, however, we become new creatures. Anything becomes possible. Although God has not yet created a new heaven and a new earth, He created us to be like Him "in true righteousness and holiness" (Eph. 4:24, NIV), and He has not given up on that. He is in the business of making new men and women. Jesus died that we might no longer live for ourselves. He wants to live His life in us, and thus to make us Life-givers.

One of those wonderful nature programs on public television showed the marvelous story of the emperor penguin of the Antarctic. The *males* incubate the eggs. I will not soon forget the scene—acres and acres of ice, surrounded by the frigid sea and a nearly black sky; wind whistling across the desolate expanse on which stood, still as statues, thousands of father penguins, each holding on top of his feet a single egg, protected by a flap of warm feathers. *They stood for three months.* By the time the chick pecked its way out of the egg, the father had nearly starved to death. At this point the mother took over the care of the chick until the father had found food in the ocean, whereupon they took turns babysitting as long as the chick needed them.

What a picture of fatherhood that is. Patience. Sacrifice.

Responsibility. Protection. Provision. That is what fathers are for. They *beget* children, but that is only the beginning. The prophet Hosea pictures the father loving his children, calling them to godliness, teaching them to walk, taking them in his arms, leading them with bonds of love, lifting them to his cheek, bending down to feed them. Of God he writes, "In thee the fatherless find a father's love" (Hos. 14:3, NEB).

I think of my own tall, spare, rather reticent, but very dear father, and how he would hold his tiny newborn in his two big hands (I remember the births of three of my siblings). I think of how he took us for walks on Saturday afternoons; got down on hands and knees and let two of us ride him like a horse around the dining room, or allowed us to sit, clasping his calves, on top of his size twelve feet as he strode around the room. In him we found a father's love.

St. Paul was a spiritual father to many. The Corinthians were his "dear children." "You may have ten thousand tutors in Christ, but you have only one father. For in Christ Jesus you are my offspring" (1 Cor. 4:15, NEB). To the Thessalonians he wrote, "We dealt with you one by one, as a father deals with his children, appealing to you by encouragement, as well as by solemn injunctions, to live lives worthy of the God who calls you into his kingdom and glory" (1 Thess. 2:11, NEB).

Scripture has very strong things to say about fathers who fail to take responsibility for their children. Eli, who had been a judge over Israel for forty years, had never judged his own sons. The child Samuel, his servant in the temple, was sent to him with a message from God: "You are to tell him that my judgment on his house shall stand for ever because he knew of his sons' blasphemies against God and did not rebuke them" (1 Sam. 3:13, NEB). The two sons were killed in battle, the Ark of God was taken, and this news was the death of old Eli.

Many readers have not known a godly and loving father. Many (such as my daughter) have not known a father at all. Yet we have the biblical pictures of fatherhood to show us what it is meant to be.

While the fathers of families have a clear and unavoidable responsibility for their children in the flesh, ought not all Christian men to think of themselves as in some measure spiritually responsible for others? May they opt out of fatherly care just because they have no biologically begotten children? Is not God calling them to forsake selfishness and to cease to live for themselves? What does this mean for fathers of families? What does it mean for single men—have they not a special responsibility to sacrifice themselves in ways married men are not free to do?

Look at J.O. Fraser who went to southwest China at the age of twenty-two and gave himself for the Lisu tribespeople, picking them up in his arms, as it were, and carrying them as a father carries his children. He was not married until he had passed forty, yet lived a life of patience, sacrifice, responsibility, protection, and provision for those people who had never before heard of Christ. It was a very lonely life for the only foreigner many of the people had ever seen. For months at a time he traveled on foot or muleback to almost unreachable villages perched high in the snowy mountains. Fraser willingly received his loneliness and his singleness as part of the price of being a servant of the Lord. It was his daily offering.[1]

And what of spiritual mothers? Anna, an old widow when

Jesus was born, spent all of her time in the temple, worshipping day and night, fasting, and praying. What greater work could she have done than thus to give herself for the life of the world? Think of Lottie Moon of China, Malla Moe and Mary Slessor of Africa, Ida Scudder and Amy Carmichael of India—single women, all of them, lonely women, no doubt. But their loneliness accepted meant life for thousands. I could name at least five women, unknown to the world, who have been Life-givers to me—three of them single, two of them widows. They would not have been free to take me to their hearts as completely as they did had they not been alone. They were mothers indeed, nurturers, vessels bearing the life of Jesus. This privilege is not beyond any woman who will give herself wholly to God.

Spiritual mothering was not, in fact, beyond even the apostle Paul. His desire to see the Galatian Christians grow up spiritually was so strong that he actually used a maternal metaphor to describe it: He "travailed in birth" for them. Moses complained to God that he had to nurse the Israelites along as though he were their mother.

The spiritual fatherhood and motherhood I speak of does not always mean that one is the instrument of another's first coming to Christ, as Paul was of some whom he fathered. Bishops, priests, elders, deacons, and deaconesses are the "parents" of the Church, the watchers, the protectors, the caregivers, the ones who lay down their lives as the servants of all. Think of the potential in the middle-aged women, married and mothers, who are lonely because their own children have gone. If instead of acceding to the usual pressure to do something for themselves "for a change," they would see the need of the young woman next door whose heart cries out for mothering, or give themselves as volunteers in hospitals and nursing homes where much lonelier women long for companionship, they would be surprised at how the words of Isaiah would come true: "If you ... satisfy the needs of the wretched, then your light will rise like dawn out of darkness and ... the Lord ... will satisfy your needs...; will give you strength of limb; you will be like a well-watered garden, like a spring whose waters never fail" (Isa. 58:9-11, NEB).

Chapter Twenty-Five

An Exchanged Life

In the southeastern United States there are hundreds of women who have been mothered by one single woman who gave up her job at Auburn University in order to teach them the Bible, to be available to them when they needed her, to lay down her life. She is Betty Thomas, one of the most unassuming and selfless people I know.

"You can pick out her disciples," a friend of hers said to me. "They're different. There is a mark on them—the mark of godliness which they have learned from Betty." It's true. I have seen that mark myself.

Last week at a conference in Boston a middle-aged woman whose name I have already forgotten said to me, "I'm an available woman. That's my job. When people ask what I do, I just say I'm an available woman." I asked if she ever found herself out of a job. Laughter was her only response. No doubt laughter has been the response of some of those who have heard her job description, but she does the job for God, not for the prestige.

The choice to become parents is a choice to be burden-bearers. Motherhood can change a giddy girl into a sober woman very quickly. Fatherhood means taking on the frightening demands of providing for totally dependent people. It means being willing to give up a good many hobbies and pastimes, the guarantee of an unbroken night's sleep, the ease of coming and going when you please. It means a willingness to change a diaper (yes, even one that isn't only wet), take out the garbage, read a bedtime story, lug the potty chair and the playpen and the carseat all over the place. It means using a whole lot of skills you haven't got, and not using the ones you know you've got. A friend who has experience in one rather prestigious field and is now working in a much humbler one wrote to me of the joy of knowing she is where God put her. But sometimes there's a nagging little voice that reminds her that she isn't "using her skills." I quoted her to my sister-in-law, whose response was, "Good training for motherhood!"

The spiritual analogies are plain. The choice to become a spiritual parent is a choice to lose one's life. It is a choice to become a burden-bearer. Spiritual dependents are a disruption and a burden. The prospect is daunting, and the greater our appreciation of such a high calling, the greater our sense of inadequacy.

"High expectations can always be crippling," writes a middle-aged bachelor, ruminating on the postponing of marriage and family.

I don't want to be slipshod or inadequate, aloof or overbearing; I don't want to ... accept tasks that I will do poorly. And so I stop at the pool's edge, computing the water's depth, dipping a toe for the temperature, and premeditating, appraising, forming opinions, being practical and praiseworthy, while others very happily swim or pitifully sink. How to explain, otherwise, my ambivalence, my inability to say *yes, of course* to the issue of marrying and having children after so many paragraphs than to say that I am overawed by the importance and permanence and risk of the issue?[1]

What God calls us to do is always impossible. Impossible, that is, without His help. It is always too big for us, too demanding. The price is too high. Yet He calls us to count not our lives dear to ourselves. Fathers and mothers haven't much time to think about the impossibilities. They must simply do the job. They haven't much time to think about loneliness, either.

It is heartening to find that even in a time when so many seem to be living wholly for themselves, there are men who not only do not shrink from the prospect of fatherhood, they long for it. Harry Stein of *Esquire* magazine writes of

conflict between the imperatives of career and those of parenting—in a fuller sense, between achievement on the world's terms and on one's own....

On the one hand, what I have with my children is priceless beyond measure; those thousands of hours on the floor amidst blocks and puzzle pieces and assorted dollies, of passing on the wisdom of Johanna Spyri and Dr. Seuss, of concocting games and stories and songs of our own, and simply sitting around not doing much at all, have been the most gratifying, the most emotionally stimulating of my life. On the other hand ... there are times when the price paid for them seems so terribly high. The fact is, since the arrival of my daughter, three and a half years ago, I have been nowhere near as productive professionally as I'd otherwise have been, as I once was.... It is hard not to regret ... being considerably less far along in what Horatio Alger would call "the game of life" than I once supposed I'd now be.[2]

He goes on to declare that the exchange has been so overwhelmingly favorable that "the perceived downside hardly bears mentioning at all." In fact, he says in conclusion, he would not trade it for an armful of Nobel Prizes.

I have four brothers. None has made a pile of money, but all have gained riches of another kind. All are fathers—both physically and spiritually. Phil, the oldest, father of two, has been a missionary in Northwest Territory for more than thirty-five years. He began in an out-of-the-way place called Nahanni where he and his diminutive southern wife built a log cabin and traveled by dog sled in order to learn an unwritten Indian language so that they could give the Gospel to people who did not have it.

Dave, father of four, was a missionary in Costa Rica and Colombia and lives now in Singapore as director of the World Evangelical Fellowship. I meet his spiritual offspring frequently in my travels.

Tom, father of two, is a writer and a teacher. In secondary schools and colleges, in England and the United States, he has spiritually "fathered" young people, trying to impart to them a wider and more glorious Christian vision.

Jim, father of four, is the youngest. He is an artist, and the pastor of a small church in a small city—Cody, Wyoming.

This answers the question of what they do professionally. It tells nothing of the spiritual fathering each has been doing. I don't suppose any of them has thought of it especially in this way. I have never asked them. But I see it. I know it's what they do. I also know a little bit about the loneliness life has dealt out to them, though I've never heard one of them mention the word. They are men. Each has taken on responsibilities beyond their families and their jobs which have meant *my life for yours.*

Chapter Twenty-six

A Gate of Hope

This book is dedicated to Katherine Morgan whom I met in New York City in 1952 when she had brought her four daughters home from Colombia for high school. She worked for a missionary magazine called *Voices,* in a tiny office in a dismal building near City Hall. I sometimes helped her there, doing odd jobs for the staff—consisting of Katherine, one or two other women (if my memory is correct), and the superannuated editor.

We usually ate lunch in the office, making tea in a seedy little washroom and sometimes feasting on cold mutton pies brought in by the editor, a Scot, who thought even the solidified fat delectable. I plied Katherine with questions about her life—her experiences as missionary, wife, mother, widow. She answered them always with good humor and often downright hilarity. When I probed things most of us would call problems she made light of them.

One day, in answer to a question, she said, "I'm sure I'm a

better woman because I'm a widow than I would have been otherwise."

She was unfailingly thoughtful and kind to the old man she worked under; she took time for me, a hopeful missionary candidate (and more or less "booted" me to South America); she laid down her life daily for more than half a century in Pasto and then in Bogotá. She kept open house for anybody and everybody—the poor, the sorrowing, the ill; the insane, the outcasts and criminals, the dying. Anyone who needed a mother and a home and love found them all at Katherine's. She did it not merely unselfishly. She did it with no thought of self whatsoever.

Her Valley of Baca (weeping) was made a place of springs for me and for thousands of Colombians. For me she stood as irrefutable proof that the answer to our loneliness is *love*—not our finding someone to love us, but our surrendering to the God who has always loved us with an everlasting love. Loving Him is then expressed in a happy and full-hearted pouring out of ourselves in love to others.

I'm still behind Katherine and all the rest who have so brightly shown me this pathway to God. I'm praying and trusting that the same Lord who drew them after Himself will keep on drawing me. We have His promise, "I will woo her, I will go with her into the wilderness and comfort her: there I will restore her vineyards, turning the Vale of Trouble into the Gate of Hope" (Hos. 2:14-15, NEB).

Notes

TWO
Fierceness and Tenderness

1. Paul Tillich, *The Eternal Now* (New York: Scribner, 1963), 15, 16.
2. Gerald Vann, *The Son's Course* (Glasgow: Collins, 1960), 10.

SIX
The Gift of Widowhood

1. The story of those years is told in *Shadow of the Almighty, Passion and Purity,* and *These Strange Ashes.*
2. C.S. Lewis, *The Problem of Pain* (New York: Macmillan, 1965), 35.

SEVEN
Under the Same Auspices

1. Amy Carmichael, *Kohila* (London: Society for Promoting Christian Knowledge, 1939), 111.

NINE
A Love Strong Enough to Hurt

1. See Luke 20:18; Dan. 6:20; Ezek. 37:3; 2 Kings 18:35; 1 Kings 17:20; 2 Kings 6:15, 6:33; John 6:15, 3:4, 4:11, 6:52, 7:15, 6:9; Mark 16:3.

TEN
Death Is a New Beginning

1. Lilias Trotter, *Parables of the Cross* (London: Algiers Mission Board and North Africa Mission, 1964), 24–25.

ELEVEN
The Price Is Outrageous

1. Joseph Conrad, *The Mirror of the Sea* (Garden City, N.Y.: Doubleday, Page, and Co., 1916), 16–17.
2. Perè Didon, *Spiritual Letters,* as quoted in Amy Carmichael, *Gold Cord* (London: Society for Promoting Christian Knowledge, 1932), 58–59.
3. See Luke 14:31.
4. Quoted in Gerald Vann's *The Son's Course* (Glasgow: Collins, 1960), 128.

TWELVE
The Intolerable Compliment

1. C.S. Lewis, *The Problem of Pain* (New York: Macmillan, 1965), 41.
2. Gerard Manley Hopkins, "The Golden Echo," in *Poems and Prose of Gerard Manley Hopkins,* Selected With an Introduction and Notes by W.H. Gardner, ed. (Harmondsworth, Middlesex: Penguin, 1960), 53, 54.

THIRTEEN
Married but Alone

1. Tillich, 17.
2. Ruth Sanford, *Do You Feel Alone in the Spirit?* (Ann Arbor: Servant, 1978).
3. I am indebted to C.S. Lewis or George MacDonald, perhaps both, for the idea of these last two sentences.
4. Quoted in Walker Percy's Foreword to *The New Catholics,* ed. Dan O'Neill (New York: Crossroad, 1987).

FOURTEEN
Love Means Acceptance

1. See Job 1:9-11.
2. See Job 42:5-6.
3. Maud Monahan, *The Life and Letters of Janet Erskine Stuart* (London: Longmans, Green & Co., 1953), 97.
4. Amy Carmichael, "For in Acceptance Lieth Peace," in *Toward Jerusalem* (Copyright 1936, Dohnavur Fellowship). Published by Christian Literature Crusade, Inc., Ft. Washington, Pennsylvania, 40. Reprinted by permission.

FIFTEEN
A Field With a Treasure in It

1. Robert Service, "The Law of the Yukon," in *Collected Poems of Robert Service* (New York: Dodd, Mead, & Co., 1940), 10.
2. Vann, 92.
3. *The Letters of Samuel Rutherford* (Chicago: Moody Press, 1951), 129.

SIXTEEN
Make Me a Cake

1. For a fuller treatment of these offerings, see Elisabeth Elliot, *Discipline: The Glad Surrender* (Old Tappan, N.J.: Revell, 1985).
2. Amy Carmichael, "Nothing in the House," in *Toward Jerusalem* (Copyright 1936, Dohnavur Fellowship). Published by Christian Literature Crusade, Inc., Ft. Washington, Pennsylvania, 44.

SEVENTEEN
The Glory of Sacrifice

1. See 1 Peter 2:5.
2. From "A Penitential Order: Rite One," in The Book of Common Prayer, 1979.
3. Ps. 57:2, NEB; Ps. 40:5, NEB; Ps. 119:91, NEB; Rom 8:28, PHILLIPS; Eph. 1:11-12, NEB; 2 Cor. 5:5, NEB.

NINETEEN
A Strange Peace

1. St. Julian of Norwich.
2. Rumer Godden, *In This House of Brede* (New York: Viking, 1969), 3.

TWENTY
Help Me Not to Want So Much

1. For more on the natural craving for human love, see Elisabeth Elliot, *Passion and Purity* (Old Tappan, N.J.: Revell, 1984).

TWENTY-ONE
Turn Your Solitude Into Prayer

1. Albert Camus, *The Fall* (New York: Alfred A. Knopf, 1957), 133.

2. Siegfried Sassoon, "Alone," in *Modern American and British Poetry,* by Louis Untermeyer, published for United States Armed Forces by Harcourt, Brace & Co. (no city given), 2: 344. Copyright Siegfried Sassoon; reprinted by kind permission of George Sassoon.

TWENTY-TWO
How Do I Do This Waiting Stuff?

1. From the New English Bible and the Jerusalem Bible.
2. From *A Litany for the Personal Life,* adapted by Charles David Williams, 13th printing (Cincinnati: Forward Movement Publications, n.d.).

TWENTY-THREE
A Pathway to Holiness

1. George Herbert, "A Dialogue Anthem," in *The Poems of George Herbert* (London: Oxford, 1958), 153.

TWENTY-FOUR
Spiritual Maturity Means Spiritual Parenthood

1. See Eileen Crossman, *Mountain Rain* (Singapore: Overseas Missionary Fellowship, 1984).

TWENTY-FIVE
An Exchanged Life

1. Ron Hanson, "The Male Clock," *Esquire,* April 1985.
2. Harry Stein, "A Man of Progeny," *Esquire,* April 1985.